Also by Sally Sampson

PARTY NUTS!

THE BAKE SALE COOKBOOK

THE OCCIDENTAL TOURIST
(*with Stan Frankenthaler*)

THE OLIVES DESSERT TABLE
(*with Todd English and Paige Retus*)

THE $50 DINNER PARTY

THE FIGS TABLE
(*with Todd English*)

THE OLIVES TABLE
(*with Todd English*)

THE DIET WORKSHOP'S
RECIPES FOR HEALTHY LIVING
(*with Lois L. Lindauer*)

CHIC SIMPLE COOKING
(*with Kim Gross, et al.*)

Souped Up!

MORE THAN 100 RECIPES FOR
SOUPS, STEWS, AND CHILIS,
AND THE BREADS,
SALADS, AND SWEETS
TO MAKE THEM
A MEAL

Sally Sampson

SIMON & SCHUSTER
New York London Toronto Sydney Singapore

SIMON & SCHUSTER
Rockefeller Center
1230 Avenue of the Americas
New York, NY 10020

For information regarding special discounts for bulk purchases,
please contact Simon & Schuster Special Sales:
1-800-456-6798 or business@simonandschuster.com

Designed and illustrated by Jill Weber

Manufactured in the United States of America

10   9   8   7   6   5   4   3   2   1

Library of Congress Cataloging-in-Publication Data
Sampson, Sally, 1955–
Souped up : more than 100 recipes for soups, stews, and chilis,
and the breads, salads, and sweets to make them a meal /
Sally Sampson.
p. cm.
Includes index.
1. Soups. 2. Stews. I. Title.

TX757.S26 2003
641.8'13—dc21   2002030670

ISBN 0-7432-2597-X

Acknowledgments

As always, thanks, gratitude,

and affection for Sydny Miner,

Carla Glasser, and Jenny Alperen,

and to Keri Fisher, who helped

with the details

For Benjamin, Lauren, and Mark

Contents

Breads to Make It a Meal   176

Seven Perfect Sweets   183

Souped Up!

Introduction

I have never had such a hard time completing a cookbook. This one, my eleventh, is a book that could easily never have been finished. The possible and probable variations are endless. What I love about cooking soup is its versatility and forgiveness (good qualities in almost anything or anyone).

There is absolutely no food I enjoy cooking more than soup (in fact, I have some of Gordon Hamersley's lentil soup simmering on the stove right now). I cook it constantly. I especially like to make it in the cold, cold winter, when no small part of the appeal is fogging the windows, but I also love to make it in the summer. I like to make it when I am angry (but not too angry) or blue, but should I find a really beautiful squash or some perfectly ripe tomatoes, well, then, I would have to say I love to make soup when I feel joy, too.

I love to eat soup and I love to make soup. On both counts, it makes me feel virtuous. Cooking soup is a great way to be creative with seasonal ingredients, feed a crowd, even to relieve anxiety. I am especially fond of making soup as a way of cleaning out my pantry and/or my refrigerator. Soup works for those who want to put on weight, and for those who want to take it off. It can be an entire meal, a starter, a dessert. It can be served for dinner, lunch, or even breakfast. It is the original comfort food: It is great for children, those who are sick, and those who have overindulged. In short, soup cures whatever ails you.

Please Read Before Proceeding

The recipes in this book are extremely doable, use easily purchased ingredients, and are not time consuming to prepare. They have been tested hundreds of times by myself and others. I know they work.

★ For the best texture, use a blender rather than a food processor when pureeing soups. The blender emulsifies the soup, whereas the food processor chops it to death.

★ When adding hot broth to the blender, start with a small amount of solids and blend at the lowest speed. Gradually add liquid and increase the speed.

★ Use ladles.

★ Buy an OXO vegetable peeler: it doesn't get any better than that.

★ Most important, use these recipes as guidelines; feel free to improvise.

On Ingredients and Amounts

When I first envisioned this book, I thought back on all my years of making soup for my takeout shop in Brookline: We made massive amounts of soup in very few steps. All my shop recipes used unpeeled ingredients like whole broccoli heads and zucchini, whole cans of whole tomatoes, unpeeled whole potatoes (I do, however, peel carrots unless they are *very* clean, in which case I scrub them). I hated to have little bits of things filling the refrigerator or, for that matter, the sink. And I still do.

It was with these methods in mind that I wrote this book. In the recipes, I rarely specify cups, preferring to call for whole potatoes, whole carrots, whole onions. I generally use red potatoes, which I do not peel; I like the flecks of color. I do not peel or seed tomatoes; I like their texture. Unless otherwise specified, all the soups are cooked uncovered.

My goal is for you to feel the freedom to adjust accordingly. Do not get caught up in precision; making soup calls for—no, it demands—flexibility. If you find that a soup is too thick because, for example, the broccoli head is larger than expected, simply add more stock or more cream.

If this is too general and you want more explicit guidelines, here are some general equivalents:

ASPARAGUS—1 pound, trimmed and peeled=3 to 3½ cups
    trimmed, peeled, and chopped
BROCCOLI—1 average head=1½ to 1¾ pounds, or 4½ to 5 cups
    chopped
BROCCOLI RABE—1 pound=4 cups chopped
BUTTERNUT SQUASH—1 large=2 to 2½ pounds, or 5 cups
    chopped
CARROTS—1 medium=⅙ pound or ¾ cup

CAULIFLOWER—1 medium head=2 to 2½ pounds, or 5 to 6 cups chopped

CELERIAC—1 large=1 pound, or 4 to 4½ cups

CELERY—1 bunch=12 to 14 stalks, or 1¾ to 2 pounds

CORN—1 medium ear=½ cup

CUCUMBER—1 medium=½ pound

EGGPLANT—1 medium=1 to 1½ pounds, or 6 cups

KALE—1 pound=5 to 7 cups chopped

LEEKS—1 average bunch=4 to 5 leeks, or 2 pounds untrimmed

MUSHROOMS—1 pound=6 to 7 cups trimmed and sliced

PARSNIPS—1 medium=⅕ pound, or ½ to ¾ cup

PEPPERS, BELL—1 medium=⅓ pound

POTATOES—1 medium or 4 small=½ pound, or 2 cups diced

PUMPKIN—1 medium=5 pounds

SPANISH ONION—1 large=¾ pound, or 1½ to 2 cups

SPINACH—1 pound=8 to 9 cups chopped

SWEET POTATOES—1 medium=½ to ¾ pound, or 2 to 2½ cups diced

SUMMER SQUASH—1 medium=½ pound, or 1½ to 2 cups diced

TOMATOES—1 medium=½ pound

TURNIPS—1 pound=4 cups chopped

WATERCRESS—1 pound=3½ cups chopped

ZUCCHINI—1 medium=½ pound, or 1¾ cups sliced

METRIC EQUIVALENCIES

CUSTOMARY	METRIC	CUSTOMARY	METRIC
¼ teaspoon	1.25 milliliters	1 pint (*2 cups*)	480 milliliters
½ teaspoon	2.5 milliliters	1 quart (*4 cups, 32 ounces*)	960 milliliters (*.96 liter*)
1 teaspoon	5 milliliters		
1 tablespoon	15 milliliters	1 gallon (*4 quarts*)	3.84 liters
1 fluid ounce	30 milliliters	1 ounce (*by weight*)	28 grams
¼ cup	60 milliliters	¼ pound (*4 ounces*)	114 grams
⅓ cup	80 milliliters	1 pound (*16 ounces*)	454 grams
½ cup	120 milliliters	2.2 pounds	1 kilogram (*1,000 grams*)
1 cup	240 milliliters		

Essential Ingredients

There are a few ingredients that are essential to soup making. If you have these on hand, you can always make *some* kind of soup.

IN THE PANTRY

CANNED
Black turtle beans
Kidney beans, dark red (I hate the pale ones)
Tomatoes, crushed
Tomatoes, diced
Tomatoes, whole peeled Italian plum
White cannellini beans

DRY GOODS
Black turtle beans
Boxed chicken stock (I like the Pacific brand, available in whole-food stores)
Brown rice
Lentils
Navy beans
Oils: olive, safflower, canola
Orzo
Pasta, various shapes and sizes
Split peas
Sun-dried tomatoes
Vinegar: red wine, balsamic, Sherry
White cannellini beans
White rice

ALCOHOL
Ale, beer
Cognac
Dry red wine
Dry Sherry
Dry white wine

FRUITS AND VEGETABLES
Carrots
Celery
Garlic
Lemons
Limes
Potatoes
Red onions
Scallions
Shallots
Spanish onions
Tomatoes

FREEZER
Bacon
Cut-up chicken
Unsalted butter

DRIED HERBS AND SPICES

The quality of the herbs and spices you use, whether dried or fresh, is absolutely critical to successful soup making. I usually use dried herbs at the beginning (they stand up better to long cooking) and fresh herbs at the end.

Buy small amounts. Both herbs and ground spices decrease in potency with time, and with exposure to air and sunlight.

Basil

Bay leaves

Cayenne

Chili powder

Cinnamon

Crushed red-pepper flakes

Cumin

Curry powder*

Greek oregano

Hungarian paprika

Marjoram

Nutmeg

Rosemary

Sage

Thyme

FRESH HERBS

Most grocery and produce stores now carry a full array of fresh herbs, even in the winter. I use Italian flat-leaf parsley, basil, and rosemary the most.

Cilantro must be used fresh. The dried form is called *coriander* and the taste is very different. If you cannot find fresh cilantro skip any recipe calling for it.

★ A note about curry powder: Purists insist that you grind your own curry powder; I have tried to do this and I must admit that I have not been able to make one that I like as well as those I have purchased. It is important not to get too carried away—leave some things to the experts.

Essential Equipment

Before I opened up my shop on Harvard Street I worked at Crate & Barrel, known for selling great housewares and cooking equipment. When I worked there I was absolutely unable to sell food processors or any other machines, because I was convinced that the joy of cooking came from the hands-on process. After having chopped literally tons of vegetables and whipped dozens and dozens of eggs by hand, I have changed my tune. While I still cherish my knives, I worship my food processor.

Making soup can be as complicated or as simple as you wish; most soups can be made with a knife and a cutting board. I use a blender most often, and am not a fan of either food mills or immersion blenders but I have to admit that I like the *idea* of both. However, should you want or require ease, I have included my preferences and recommendations. In many cases, I recommend particular brands and name them, because time and experience have taught me that, while it often makes sense to buy the most expensive item, often it does not. I have bought equipment of the most utilitarian sort and been happy, and I have bought equipment just to have something beautiful to look at. The first is a matter of experience; the second, taste. My hope is that this list will prevent you from having to replace pieces you buy now with different pieces later.

> Heavy-bottomed 4-quart and 6-quart stockpots (Calphalon, All Clad, or le Creuset)
> Food processor (Cuisinart or Kitchen Aid)
> Blender (Oster)
> Strainer or colander
> Assorted ladles: 4 ounce, 6 ounce
> Assorted wooden spoons

Good knives
Vegetable peeler (OXO)
Pepper mill
Corkscrew
Measuring cups and spoons (OXO)
Whisks
Graters

Stocks

*I*t is perhaps heresy to say so, but I think that the importance of making your own stock has been greatly overrated.

The culinary world's insistence on *making* stock has prevented many otherwise gifted would-be soup makers from making soup. There are many stocks, broths, and soup bases on the market that are excellent. Some have MSG, some do not. Some have salt, some do not. Choosing which is right for you is a matter of personal taste. I will not intentionally eat anything with MSG in it, and I know that a lot of people are allergic to it; it is something to watch out for. Many specialty and whole food stores carry chicken and vegetable bases that are made without stabilizers or enhancers of any kind.

While clear and broth-like soups are somewhat better when made with homemade stock, I have found that most of the soups that I make rely less on the base and more on the flavoring of the main ingredient and/or herb.

Do try making your own stock; there is something very satisfying about the process and the results are, of course, worth the work—but only if you think that it is important, you enjoy making it, and you have the time.

The recipe for Helen Geller's Matzoh Ball Soup (page 102) makes an excellent chicken stock and the recipe for Not French Onion Soup (page 55) makes an excellent vegetable stock, as does Stan Frankenthaler's Vegetable Stock (page 4). If you're looking for a good beef stock, I recommend the recipes in Julia Child's *The Way to Cook* (Knopf, 1989) or Bernard Clayton's *The Complete Book of Soups and Stews* (Fireside, 1984).

Chicken or Turkey Stock

Louise Corrigan was my favorite editor when I wrote for The Boston Globe; *when she left to write her own book, she continued writing articles. I begged her to let me quote from this one; in fact, I told her that I was sorry I hadn't written it myself:*

"At this time of year, deep into soup season, I find myself thinking often of my grandmother's turkey soup. And whenever I do, I remember how awful it was.

"Here's the recipe: Take one turkey carcass, stripped of every last trace of edible meat. Put it in a huge pot with a limp carrot and a brownish stalk of celery. Add too much salt and twice as much water as any sensible person would use. Boil long enough to make the house smell good, but not long enough to infuse the water with any discernible taste of turkey. Ladle the brackish, faintly poultry-scented broth into bowls and serve.

"For years, I was baffled when people extolled the wonders of homemade soup. How could anyone actually enjoy, much less prefer, this tasteless bowl of nothing? Finally, I attempted my own turkey soup, and I was amazed to realize what I'd been missing. Who knew soup had flavor?"

In spite of the fact that I think homemade stock is superior to canned or boxed, in truth, I only make this stock when I have made a chicken or a turkey for dinner and have a leftover carcass to use. I usually use it when I am making chicken soup, for that is when it matters most.

Carcass and neck from 6 to 7 pound chicken or turkey
2 celery stalks, cut in half
1 parsnip, washed and halved
2 carrots, washed and halved
1 Spanish onion, quartered
2 bay leaves
1 teaspoon dried thyme
Cold water, to cover
1 teaspoon kosher salt or more, to taste

Place all the ingredients, except the salt, in a stockpot and generously cover with cold water. Cook, partially covered, over medium heat until the mixture comes to a slow boil. Lower the heat to very low and continue cooking, partially covered, for 3 hours. Do not let it boil again.

Strain and discard the solids. Transfer to a large container, cover, and refrigerate up to three days. When the stock has completely cooled, skim and discard the hardened fat. Add salt to taste. Freeze up to six months.

YIELD: ABOUT 10 CUPS

Stan Frankenthaler's Vegetable Stock

Rich and flavorful, Stan's vegetable stock can be easily substituted for chicken stock in any vegetable or bean soup.

1 tablespoon soy oil
2 large or 4 small Spanish onions, coarsely chopped
1 leek green, sliced
1 garlic bulb, halved horizontally to expose the cloves
3 carrots, coarsely chopped
1 fennel bulb, coarsely chopped
3 to 4 cups fresh white button mushrooms
4 celery stalks, sliced
16 cups (1 gallon) cold water

Place a large stockpot over medium heat and, when it is hot, add the oil. Add the onions, leeks, garlic, carrots, fennel, mushrooms, and celery, and cook until they are very tender and just starting to fall apart, about 30 minutes. Add the water and cook over high heat until it comes to a boil.

Lower the heat to low and cook until the vegetables are completely falling apart, about 30 minutes. Strain and discard the solids. Transfer to a large container, cover, and refrigerate up to three days or freeze up to six months.

YIELD: 12 CUPS

Smooth and Pureed Vegetable Soups

Vegetable soups are the easiest, most varied, and most versatile of soups. Most can be made from start to finish in less than an hour, and almost all lend themselves to creative substitutions. With the exception of tomatoes and artichokes, always use fresh vegetables, but feel free to experiment.

Asparagus with Fresh Herbs

I love asparagus soup, yet almost never order it when I am in restaurants. Instead of the typical drab, green glop they pass off as asparagus soup, this delicate version is a fresh, bright, rich green made only with straight, crisp stalks.

> WIDELY USED IN FRENCH COOKING, **TARRAGON**, A MEMBER OF THE SUNFLOWER FAMILY, HAS A SLIGHTLY BITTERSWEET ANISE FLAVOR. THERE ARE TWO CULTIVATED SPECIES OF TARRAGON, RUSSIAN AND FRENCH. TARRAGON, UNLIKE MANY OTHER HERBS, WAS USED AS A MEDICINAL DRUG UNTIL THE SIXTEENTH CENTURY, AND WAS NOT BROUGHT TO THE UNITED STATES UNTIL THE EARLY NINETEENTH CENTURY. IT WAS BELIEVED TO CURE SNAKEBITE.

Store asparagus in the refrigerator in the same way you would a bouquet of flowers: standing upright in water.

1 tablespoon unsalted butter, olive oil, or canola oil
1 Spanish onion, coarsely chopped
2 garlic cloves, pressed or finely chopped
4 to 5 cups chicken stock
2 bunches fresh asparagus, woody stems broken off and discarded, stalks and tips chopped
1 teaspoon fresh tarragon or rosemary leaves, or 2 tablespoons chopped fresh basil leaves, plus additional for garnish
½ teaspoon Dijon mustard
2 to 3 tablespoons fresh chopped chives, for garnish (optional)
Parmesan, goat, or feta cheese (optional)

Place a stockpot over medium heat and, when it is hot, add the butter or oil. Add the onion and garlic, and cook until tender and lightly colored, about 10 to 15 minutes.

Add the stock, raise the heat to high, and bring to a boil.

Add the asparagus, and when it returns to a rolling boil, remove the solids and place in a blender. Add the tarragon and Dijon mustard. Process until smooth, gradually adding the cooking liquid.

Strain the soup if you must. (Straining will get rid of the slight stringiness. This is a matter of taste.) Serve immediately, garnished with chives and Parmesan cheese.

VARIATIONS:

Cream of Asparagus: Decrease the chicken stock by ¼ to ½ cup and stir in ¼ to ½ cup heavy cream after the soup has been pureed.

Chilled Asparagus: Double the amount of mustard and tarragon, and chill for 2 hours. Garnish just before serving.

YIELD: ABOUT 5 CUPS

Broccoli Spinach

*T*wo much maligned and hotly debated vegetables come together, and bring out the best in both. Even detractors of each vegetable individually will be pleased with the resulting combination.

The one thing I hate about making this soup is cleaning the spinach which, unless previously washed, is always incredibly, incredibly sandy. I usually soak the spinach in cold water and then lift it out (as opposed to draining it) and repeat the process until the bowls have no sand left in them.

---

1 tablespoon olive oil or unsalted butter
1 Spanish onion, coarsely chopped
4 garlic cloves, thinly sliced or chopped
2 carrots, sliced
1 small head broccoli, woody end discarded, stem peeled and
    sliced, florets chopped
1 28-ounce can whole tomatoes, drained
7 cups chicken stock
2 small bunches leaf spinach or watercress, cleaned and stemmed
1 teaspoon freshly squeezed lemon juice
Lemon slices, for garnish

Place a stockpot over medium heat and, when it is hot, add the oil. Add the onion, garlic, and carrots, and cook until tender and lightly colored, about 10 to 15 minutes.

Add the broccoli stems, tomatoes, stock, and half the spinach, and bring to a boil. Lower the heat to low and cook until the stems are tender, about 15 minutes.

Add the florets and the remaining spinach and cook until the florets are just tender, about 7 to 10 minutes.

Remove the solids and place in a food processor or blender. Process until smooth, gradually adding the cooking liquid. Add the lemon juice and serve immediately, garnished with lemon slices.

VARIATION:

Cream of Broccoli Spinach: **Stir in ½ cup heavy cream after blending.**

Roasted Butternut Squash with Apples

Silky, slightly sweet, a touch hot. In short, perfect.

> ✳ **MARJORAM**, A MEMBER OF THE MINT FAMILY, HAS A DELICATE, SWEET OREGANO-LIKE FLAVOR WITH A SLIGHTLY BITTER UNDERTONE. IN FACT, FRESH MARJORAM AND OREGANO ARE PRACTICALLY IDENTICAL. EARLY GREEKS WOVE MARJORAM INTO FUNERAL WREATHS AND PLANTED IT ON GRAVES TO SYMBOLIZE THEIR LOVED ONES' HAPPINESS BOTH IN LIFE AND BEYOND. IT WAS SAID THAT IF MARJORAM GREW ON THE GRAVE OF A DEAD PERSON, HE WOULD ENJOY ETERNAL BLISS.

> ✳ FROM THE SOUTHERN INDIAN WORD *KARI*, MEANING "SAUCE," THIS TERM IS USED TO REFER TO ANY NUMBER OF HOT, SPICY, GRAVY-BASED DISHES OF EAST INDIAN ORIGIN. **CURRY POWDER** BEARS NO RELATION TO CURRY LEAVES, WHICH SMELL OF TANGERINE AND ARE RARELY FOUND OUTSIDE OF INDIA OR IN INDIAN SPECIALTY STORES. CURRY POWDER IS A BRITISH INVENTION, DESIGNED TO IMITATE THE FLAVOR OF INDIAN FOODS, AND IS A MIXTURE OF SPICES THAT MAY CONTAIN ANY OR ALL OF THE FOLLOWING: CUMIN, CORIANDER, BLACK PEPPER, CHILIES, FENUGREEK, GINGER, CINNAMON, CLOVES, CARDAMOM, AND SALT.

1 large butternut squash, peeled, seeded, and cubed
1 Granny Smith apple, peeled, if desired, and cubed
4 teaspoons olive oil
1 Spanish onion, chopped
2 garlic cloves, chopped
2 teaspoons curry powder
1 teaspoon dried basil
8 cups chicken or vegetable stock
½ cup dry white wine

Preheat the oven to 425 degrees.

Rub the squash and apple cubes with 2 teaspoons of oil, and place on a sheet pan in the oven until the squash is browned and tender, about 40 minutes.

Place a stockpot over medium heat and when it is hot, add the remaining 2 teaspoons olive oil. Add the onion, garlic, curry, and basil and cook until tender, about 10 to 15 minutes.

Add the roasted squash, apples, stock, and wine and bring to a boil. Lower the heat to medium low and cook for 20 minutes.

Transfer to a blender in batches and blend until smooth. Transfer to a container, cover, and refrigerate up to three days or serve immediately.

YIELD: 7 TO 8 CUPS

Cream of Broccoli

Another soup I never, ever order out. Most of the time, the broccoli is overcooked and loses all flavor and texture. Here, instead, the broccoli is only just-cooked, then pureed immediately to insure full flavor. Feel free to add your favorite fresh herb before serving; basil and dill are among my favorites.

1 tablespoon unsalted butter or olive or canola oil
1 Spanish onion, coarsely chopped
1 celery stalk, chopped
1 small carrot, peeled and thinly sliced
5 to 6 cups chicken stock (depending on the size of the broccoli head)
1 head broccoli, woody stems discarded, florets chopped
½ cup heavy or light cream
1 to 2 teaspoons freshly squeezed lemon juice
Kosher salt and black pepper

Place a stockpot over medium heat and, when it is hot, add the butter or oil. Add the onion, celery, and carrot and cook until tender and lightly colored, about 10 to 15 minutes.

Add the stock, raise the heat to high, and bring to a boil. While the broth is boiling, slowly add the broccoli florets. Return to a boil briefly.

Lower the heat to medium and cook until the broccoli is just tender, 5 to 8 minutes.

Remove the solids and place in a food processor or blender. Process until smooth, gradually adding the cooking liquid and the cream. Add additional stock if the soup is too thick. Add the lemon juice, salt, and pepper, and serve immediately.

YIELD: 6 TO 7 CUPS

VARIATIONS:

Broccoli with Cheese: **When you are blending, add 1 cup grated Cheddar, goat, or Swiss cheese.**

Carrot with Fennel

While I adore this smooth, creamy, and unusual soup, I am most definitely not a fan of cooked carrots.

USED AS A MEDICINAL PLANT, HERB, AND VEGETABLE, **FENNEL** IS A FLESHY, BULBLIKE VEGETABLE WITH PALE-GREEN, STRIATED STALKS. IT HAS A REFRESHING AND MILD LICORICE FLAVOR, AND IS ESPECIALLY FAVORED IN ITALIAN CUISINE.

1 tablespoon olive or canola oil
1 Spanish onion, coarsely chopped
1½ to 2 pounds carrots, peeled, if desired, and sliced
1 teaspoon dried fennel seed
8 cups chicken or vegetable stock

Place a stockpot over medium heat and, when it is hot, add the oil. Add the onion, carrots, and fennel and cook until tender and lightly colored, about 10 to 15 minutes.

Add the stock, raise the heat to high, and bring to a boil. Lower the heat to low and cook until the carrots are tender, about 20 minutes.

Remove the solids and place in a food processor or blender. Process until smooth, gradually adding the cooking liquid. Transfer to a container, cover, and refrigerate up to three days, or serve immediately.

YIELD: 8 TO 10 CUPS

VARIATIONS:

You can omit the fennel seed and add 2 tablespoons basil, cilantro, or chives (or all three) at the end, just prior to blending or serving.

Cauliflower Cilantro

Like carrots, I love cauliflower when raw but hate it cooked, unless it's in soup. In fact, its subtle flavor and smooth, silky texture make it one of my favorite starring ingredients for soup. A magical melding of ingredients, this soup tastes neither like cauliflower nor cilantro.

2 teaspoons olive oil
1 Spanish onion, chopped
2 garlic cloves, sliced
1 teaspoon ground coriander
1 head cauliflower, cored, florets coarsely chopped
8 cups chicken or vegetable stock
2 teaspoons Dijon mustard
4 tablespoons chopped fresh cilantro leaves, plus additional whole leaves for garnish

Place a stockpot over medium heat and, when it is hot, add the oil. Add the onion, garlic, and coriander and cook until tender and lightly colored, about 10 to 15 minutes.

Add the cauliflower and stock and bring to a boil. Lower the heat to low, and cook until the cauliflower is tender, about 20 to 25 minutes.

Add the mustard and cilantro and transfer the soup, in batches, to a blender. Blend until smooth. Serve immediately, garnished with whole fresh cilantro leaves.

YIELD: ABOUT 10 CUPS

Butternut Squash with Pear, Orange, and Rosemary

Smooth, slightly sweet, and subtle, this is the quintessential fall soup and a perfect starter for a Thanksgiving meal (if you can spare the room in your refrigerator or stomach).

USED SINCE 500 B.C., **ROSEMARY** IS NATIVE TO THE MEDITER-RANEAN AREA (WHERE IT GROWS WILD), BUT IS NOW CULTIVATED THROUGHOUT EUROPE AND THE UNITED STATES. ROSEMARY IS THE HARD, NEEDLE-SHAPED LEAF OF A SMALL EVERGREEN SHRUB. IT HAS A WOODSY AROMA AND A STRONG BITTERSWEET FLAVOR, WITH HINTS OF BOTH LEMON AND PINE. IN ANCIENT TIMES, THIS MEMBER OF THE MINT FAMILY WAS USED TO TREAT AILMENTS OF THE NERVOUS SYSTEM.

2 teaspoons olive oil
1 Spanish onion, chopped
1 butternut squash, peeled, seeded, and sliced
1 pear, sliced
1 sprig fresh rosemary or 1 teaspoon dried
6 to 7 cups chicken or vegetable stock
½ cup orange juice
2 to 3 teaspoons grated fresh orange zest
Orange slices, for garnish

Place a stockpot over medium heat and, when it is hot, add the oil. Add the onion and cook until tender and lightly colored, about 10 to 15 minutes.

Add the remaining ingredients, raise the heat to high, and bring to a boil. Lower the heat to low and cook, partially covered, until the squash is tender, about 25 minutes.

Transfer the solids to a blender or food processor fitted with a steel blade and process until smooth, gradually adding the cooking liquid.

Transfer to a container, cover, and refrigerate up to three days, or serve immediately, garnished with orange slices.

YIELD: ABOUT 12 CUPS

Artichoke Lemon

I am not really sure if the joy of eating artichokes comes from the work involved in getting out all the little bits, or if it is the little bits themselves. It is probably a combination. For anyone who likes the little bits—the actual flavor—this elegant, creamy, creamless soup is heavenly. I originally made it with canned artichoke bottoms, simply because I ordered them by mistake and decided, out of necessity, to put them to use. Almost twenty years and pots and pots of soup later, my childhood pal Lizzy Shaw discovered frozen artichoke bottoms at a local Armenian market. Of course, either canned or frozen will do, but I now prefer using frozen, since I am not about to use fresh.

DO NOT USE AN **ALUMINUM POT** TO MAKE THIS SOUP. PLAIN ALUMINUM FINISHES CAN DARKEN AND PIT WHEN EXPOSED TO ALKALINE OR MINERAL-RICH FOODS, AND WHEN SOAKED EXCESSIVELY IN SOAPY WATER. THEY CAN ALSO DISCOLOR SOME FOODS CONTAINING EGGS, WINE, OR OTHER ACIDIC INGREDIENTS. THIS DISCOLORATION, THOUGH NOT HARMFUL, IS UNATTRACTIVE.

A ***ROUX,*** PRONOUNCED "ROO," IS A MIXTURE OF FLOUR AND FAT USED TO THICKEN SOUPS AND SAUCES. THE FLOUR AND BUTTER ARE SLOWLY COOKED OVER LOW HEAT TO THE DESIRED SHADE OF WHITE, BLOND, OR BROWN. THE DARKER THE ROUX, THE LONGER IT HAS BEEN COOKED AND, THEREFORE, THE STRONGER AND NUTTIER THE FLAVOR.

¼ cup unsalted butter
6 garlic cloves, pressed or finely chopped
¼ cup all-purpose flour
6 cups chicken stock
2 14-ounce bags frozen artichoke bottoms
Juice of 1 lemon

Black pepper

2 tablespoons fresh basil leaves, or 1 sprig fresh thyme, for garnish
(optional)

Grated Parmesan cheese or crumbled goat cheese, for garnish
· (optional)

Place a heavy-bottomed non-aluminum stockpot over low heat and, when it is hot, add the butter. Add the garlic and cook until just golden, about 3 to 5 minutes. Add the flour very slowly and cook until it forms a thick paste, whisking all the while.

Gradually add the stock and artichoke bottoms, continuing to whisk, raise the heat to high, and bring to a boil. Lower the heat to low and simmer for 25 to 35 minutes.

Remove the solids and transfer to a food processor or blender. Process until smooth, gradually adding the cooking liquid, lemon juice, and pepper. Transfer to a container, cover, and refrigerate up to three days, or serve immediately, garnished with basil and Parmesan cheese.

YIELD: 8 TO 9 CUPS

Potato and Celeriac

A cross between two great classics—vichyssoise and cream of celery—this combines the silky texture of vichyssoise with the earthy taste of celery root.

> ❋ **CELERIAC,** ALSO CALLED *CELERY ROOT* AND *CELERY KNOB*, IS A RATHER UGLY, ODD-SHAPED, KNOBBY, BROWN VEGETABLE THAT IS ACTUALLY THE ROOT OF A SPECIAL CELERY CULTIVATED SPECIFICALLY FOR THIS PURPOSE. IT MUST BE PEELED, AND TASTES LIKE A CROSS BETWEEN CELERY AND PARSLEY.

1 leek, green part included
1 tablespoon unsalted butter
1 garlic clove, pressed or finely chopped
1 pound celeriac, peeled and diced
½ pound potatoes, unpeeled, diced (about 2 cups)
7 to 8 cups chicken or vegetable stock
½ cup heavy cream
Finely chopped scallions (green and white parts), for garnish
Chopped fresh tarragon leaves, for garnish
Crumbled blue cheese, for garnish (optional)

Cut off root end and 3 inches of green part of leek and discard. Quarter leek lengthwise and slice thin. Soak in several changes of water, being careful to get rid of all the sand.

Place a heavy-bottomed stockpot over medium heat and, when it is hot, add the butter. When the butter has melted, add the leek and garlic and cook until tender and lightly colored, about 10 to 15 minutes.

Add the celeriac, potatoes, and stock, raise the heat to high, and bring to a boil. Lower the heat to medium and cook until tender, about 20 to 35 minutes.

Remove the solids and place in a food processor or blender. Process until completely smooth, gradually adding the cooking liquid and heavy cream.

Serve immediately, garnished with scallions, tarragon leaves, and blue cheese, if desired.

Cauliflower with Cheddar

Inspired by the best omelet I have ever had: slowly cooked, caramelized onions, combined with cauliflower and cheddar, inside perfectly cooked eggs. I thought the omelet was good, but this is even better!

2 tablespoons unsalted butter
1 large Spanish onion, coarsely chopped
½ teaspoon sugar
1 head cauliflower, core removed, florets coarsely chopped
6 cups chicken stock
½ to ¾ cup grated extra-sharp Cheddar cheese
Black pepper, to taste
Chopped fresh dill or basil, for garnish
Finely chopped scallions (white and green parts), for garnish

Place a heavy-bottomed stockpot over medium heat and, when it is hot, add the butter. When the butter has melted, add the onion and sugar and cook until the onion has caramelized, about 15 to 20 minutes.

Add the cauliflower and stock, raise the heat to high, and bring to a boil. Lower the heat to low and cook until the cauliflower is tender, about 20 to 25 minutes.

Remove the solids and place in a food processor or blender. Process until smooth, gradually adding the cheese, pepper, and cooking liquid.

Serve immediately, garnished with chopped dill and scallions.

YIELD: 8 CUPS

Triple Tomato

I grew up eating and loving Campbell's Cream of Tomato soup, so when I decided to make my own tomato soup, it was that texture and flavor I had in mind. Triple tomato is perfect for adults and children who don't like too much "green stuff" in their soup, but a little more intense to please those who want something more.

> ✳ SOME TOMATOES THAT ARE LABELED *SUN-DRIED* ARE ACTUALLY DRIED IN THE SUN. MOST, HOWEVER, ARE DRIED IN A LOW OVEN FOR A LONG PERIOD OF TIME. THE **SUN-DRIED TOMATO** WE ALL KNOW AND LOVE IS SIMPLY A DRIED TOMATO, MUCH LIKE A RAISIN IS A DRIED GRAPE. PROLONGED EXPOSURE TO THE SUN CAUSES A FRUIT'S NATURAL MOISTURE TO EVAPORATE, LEAVING A DRY, SLIGHTLY CHEWY PRODUCT.

1 tablespoon unsalted butter

1 large Spanish onion, coarsely chopped or thinly sliced

1 garlic clove, pressed or finely chopped

1 celery stalk, peeled and sliced

½ teaspoon curry powder

1 28-ounce can Italian plum tomatoes, chopped

4 to 5 cups chicken or vegetable stock

1 teaspoon dried basil, or 1 tablespoon chopped fresh basil

¼ teaspoon brown sugar

5 sun-dried tomatoes, packed in oil or dried

10 cherry tomatoes, sliced, for garnish

Place a heavy-bottomed stockpot over medium heat and, when it is hot, add the butter. When the butter has melted, add the onion, garlic, celery, and curry powder and cook, covered, until vegetables are tender, about 10 to 15 minutes.

Add the plum tomatoes and their juices, stock, basil, and brown sugar, raise the heat to high and bring to a boil. Lower the heat to low and cook, partially covered, 1½ hours.

continued on next page

Triple Tomato (*cont.*)

Remove the solids and place in a blender. Add the sun-dried tomatoes and process until completely smooth, gradually adding the cooking liquid. Transfer to a container, cover, and refrigerate up to three days or serve immediately, garnished with cherry tomatoes.

YIELD: ABOUT 6 TO 7 CUPS

VARIATIONS:

Omit the sun-dried tomatoes, in which case you've made Double-Tomato Soup.

Cream of Triple Tomato: Decrease the chicken stock by ½ cup, and stir in ½ cup heavy cream or sour cream just prior to serving. For a lower-calorie and -fat version, use ½ cup buttermilk or nonfat yogurt.

Curried Tomato: Increase the curry to up to 2 tablespoons.

Dilled Tomato: Omit basil and curry and replace with ¼ cup chopped fresh dill.

Curried Cauliflower with Basil

Although there is no cream in this soup, you'd never guess it based on its consistency or taste. In fact, I intended to put cream in it but, after it was blended, adding cream seemed superfluous. Served with a salad, this makes a quick, great, light dinner.

1 tablespoon olive oil
1 Spanish onion, chopped
3 garlic cloves, minced
1 tablespoon minced ginger root
2 celery stalks, peeled and sliced
1½ tablespoons curry powder
1 head cauliflower, cored and coarsely chopped
6 cups chicken stock
4 tablespoons chopped basil or cilantro leaves, or a combination,
    plus additional for garnish
Kosher salt and black pepper, to taste

Place a stockpot over medium heat and, when it is hot, add the oil. Add the onion, garlic, ginger, celery, and curry powder and cook until tender, about 10 to 15 minutes. Raise the heat to high, add the cauliflower and stock, and bring to a boil. Cook until the cauliflower is tender, about 20 to 25 minutes.

Transfer to a blender in batches, add the basil, and blend until smooth. Add salt and pepper to taste. Serve immediately, garnished with additional basil leaves.

YIELD: ABOUT 8 TO 10 CUPS

Butternut Squash with Lime, Garlic, and Ginger

A few years ago, I did a lot of cooking demonstrations and often made this soup. To my surprise, a great number of people told me that they didn't like butternut squash. It seemed that if they did, then they didn't like lime, garlic, or ginger. I persevered and usually convinced them to try it. I almost always got the thumbs up because, somehow, the sum of the parts created a luscious and creamy soup with a flavor different enough from the ingredients. I, on the other hand, love all these flavors and still love the soup!

1 tablespoon unsalted butter

1 Spanish onion, coarsely chopped

4 garlic cloves, pressed or finely chopped

1 tablespoon peeled, coarsely chopped fresh ginger

1 butternut squash (approximately 2 to 2½ pounds), peeled, seeded, and chopped (5 cups)

5 cups chicken stock

Pinch sugar

¼ cup fresh lime juice

Fresh lime slices, for garnish

Place a heavy-bottomed stockpot over medium heat and, when it is hot, add the butter. When the butter has melted, add the onion, garlic, and ginger and cook until tender and lightly colored, about 10 to 15 minutes.

Add the butternut squash, stock, and sugar, raise the heat to high, and bring to a boil. Lower the heat to low and cook until the squash is very tender, about 20 to 25 minutes.

Remove the solids and place in a blender. Blend until smooth, gradually adding the cooking liquid and lime juice. Transfer to a container, cover, and refrigerate up to three days, or serve immediately, garnished with lime slices.

YIELD: 8 TO 10 CUPS

Cream Soups

Although I am generally not a fan of cream, I do make an exception here. A small amount can take a good tasting soup into a whole other realm, rendering it silky and transcendent.

Spicy Cauliflower

Reminiscent of soups found in Indian restaurants; alter the spiciness by increasing the amount of curry.

1 tablespoon olive or canola oil
1 large Spanish onion, coarsely chopped
2 garlic cloves, pressed or finely chopped
½ to 1½ teaspoons curry powder
½ teaspoon Dijon mustard
6 cups chicken stock
1 large red new potato, chopped (about 1 to 1½ cups)
1 head cauliflower, cored and coarsely chopped
½ teaspoon dried thyme
¼ teaspoon ground nutmeg
1 cup heavy cream, buttermilk, or low-fat yogurt (optional)
¼ to ½ cup sour cream or yogurt, for garnish
¼ cup chopped fresh cilantro leaves, for garnish

Place a heavy-bottomed stockpot over medium heat and, when it is hot, add the oil. Add the onions, garlic, and curry and cook until tender, about 10 to 15 minutes.

Add the mustard, stock, and potato, raise the heat to high, and bring to a boil.

Lower the heat to low and add the cauliflower, thyme, and nutmeg. Cook until the cauliflower is very tender, about 20 to 25 minutes.

Remove the solids and place in a blender. Process until completely smooth, gradually adding the cooking liquid and heavy cream.

Serve immediately, garnished with sour cream and cilantro.

YIELD: 10 CUPS

Corn Chowder

*T*his is an unbelievably filling soup. When you look at the ingredients, it may seem as if a half-pound of bacon is an obscene amount. It is, but, in my house everyone smells the bacon, then comes into the kitchen to beg for a piece or two. I have been known to start this soup with a full pound. Either way, be sure to discard all but two tablespoons of the fat for cooking the onion.

½ pound bacon
1 Spanish onion, chopped
2 potatoes, diced
½ teaspoon dried thyme
2 tablespoons all-purpose flour
5 cups chicken stock
4 cups corn kernels (about 4 to 6 ears)
½ cup heavy cream
Chopped fresh chives, for garnish

Place a heavy-bottomed stockpot over medium heat, add the bacon, and cook until golden brown, about 10 minutes. Set the bacon on a paper towel, and discard all but 2 tablespoons of the bacon fat. When the bacon has cooled, crumble or chop it.

Reheat the pot over medium heat and, when it is hot, add the onion and cook until tender, about 10 to 15 minutes. Add the potatoes and thyme and cook 5 minutes, stirring occasionally. Add the flour, stirring constantly, and cook for 1 to 2 minutes.

Slowly add the stock, 1 cup at a time, allowing the soup to come to a low boil after each addition. After it comes to a final boil, lower the heat to medium, and cook until the potatoes are tender, about 15 to 20 minutes. Add the corn and cream and cook until heated throughout, about 3 to 4 minutes.

Serve immediately, garnished with the reserved bacon and chives.

YIELD: 9 TO 10 CUPS

continued on next page

Corn Chowder (*cont.*)

VARIATION:

Add grated Cheddar cheese at the table, or fresh basil, cilantro, or chilies or any combination of the four.

Parsnip with Sour Cream and Mustard

Sweet, exotic, and surprising, this is an unusual soup that even parsnip haters will love.

> ❋ A ROOT VEGETABLE THAT WAS ORIGINALLY AS POPULAR AS THE
> POTATO, THE **PARSNIP** IS A YELLOWISH, FRUITY CARROT-LIKE
> VEGETABLE THAT IS SWEET, ALMOST CLOYINGLY SO.

1 tablespoon unsalted butter
1 Spanish onion, coarsely chopped
1 pound parsnips, peeled and sliced
5 cups chicken stock
½ to ¾ teaspoon Dijon mustard
½ cup sour cream
Sour cream or plain yogurt, for garnish

Place a heavy-bottomed stockpot over medium heat and, when it is hot, add the butter. When the butter has melted, add the onion and cook until tender and lightly colored, about 10 to 15 minutes.

Add the parsnips, stock, and mustard, raise the heat to high, and bring to a boil. Lower the heat to low and cook until the parsnips are very soft, about 25 minutes.

Remove the solids and place in a food processor or blender. Process until smooth, gradually adding the cooking liquid and sour cream.

Serve immediately, garnished with sour cream or yogurt.

YIELD: 7 CUPS

Cream of Mushroom

The classic.

1 tablespoon unsalted butter
1 Spanish onion, coarsely chopped or sliced
¾ pound fresh mushrooms, coarsely chopped, stems included
1 potato, unpeeled, diced (about 1 cup)
4 cups chicken stock
1 teaspoon dried rosemary, or 3 teaspoons chopped fresh
¼ cup dry red wine
½ cup heavy cream
Kosher salt and black pepper, to taste
Chopped fresh chives, for garnish (optional)
Parmesan or Gruyere cheese, for garnish (optional)

Place a heavy-bottomed stockpot over medium heat and, when it is hot, add the butter. When the butter has melted, add the onion and cook until tender and lightly colored, about 10 to 15 minutes.

Add the mushrooms, potato, stock, and rosemary, raise the heat to high, and bring to a boil. Lower the heat to low and cook for 30 minutes.

Remove the solids and place in a food processor or blender. Process until completely smooth, gradually adding the cooking liquid, wine, and heavy cream. Season to taste with salt and pepper. Transfer to a container, cover, and refrigerate up to three days, or serve immediately, garnished with chives and Parmesan or Gruyere, if desired.

YIELD: 6 TO 8 CUPS

VARIATION:

For a slightly sweeter soup, substitute Sherry for the red wine.

Cream of Celery

One of my clearest, fondest, warmest memories of childhood is of being sick. Strange, you might say, that being sick would even grace the list of happy times, but I was treated like a nine-year-old queen, a special angel. What I remember most vividly is my mother, in red lipstick and a Pucci-like dress, high heels clicking down the hallway, bringing me breakfast in bed and later, lunch in bed: Campbell's Cream of Celery Soup and Saltines, with Glamour and Seventeen magazines and a box of Colorforms. I didn't eat the Saltines, because I'm not a dunker, but I knew she was making the effort. She worked and, because I was sick, she stayed home to care for me.

While I have outgrown almost everything else, I still think of Cream of Celery as comforting and healing.

SHALLOTS, MEMBERS OF THE ONION FAMILY, ARE FORMED MORE LIKE GARLIC THAN ONIONS, WITH A HEAD COMPOSED OF MULTIPLE CLOVES, EACH COVERED WITH A THIN, PAPERY SKIN. SHALLOTS ARE FAVORED FOR THEIR MILD, ONION FLAVOR AND CAN BE USED IN THE SAME MANNER AS ONIONS.

THE LONG-HELD IDEA THAT EATING CELERY BURNS UP MORE CALORIES THAN THE CELERY ITSELF IS VERY, VERY APPEALING. NEW DISCOVERIES SHOW THAT CELERY ALSO CONTAINS *PHTHALIDES*, NUTRIENTS THAT LOWER LIPIDS AND HELP WARD OFF HEART DISEASE AND CANCER.

1 tablespoon unsalted butter
1 large shallot, coarsely chopped
6 scallions, including greens, thinly sliced, plus additional, for
    garnish
1 bunch celery, including heart and leaves, peeled and thinly sliced
6 cups chicken or vegetable stock

continued on next page

Cream of Celery (*cont.*)

> 1 large Idaho potato, unpeeled, cubed
> 1 teaspoon dried rosemary, or 1 tablespoon chopped fresh
> ½ teaspoon ground nutmeg
> ½ cup heavy or light cream
> Crumbled blue cheese, for garnish (optional)

Place a heavy-bottomed stockpot over medium heat and, when it is hot, add the butter. When the butter has melted, add the shallot, scallions, and celery and cook until tender and lightly colored, about 10 to 15 minutes.

Add the stock, potato, and rosemary, raise the heat to high, and bring to a boil. Lower the heat to low and simmer until the celery and potato are tender, about 25 minutes.

Remove the solids and place in a food processor or blender. Process until completely smooth, gradually adding the cooking liquid, nutmeg, and cream. Transfer to a container, cover, and refrigerate up to three days, or serve immediately, garnished with scallions and blue cheese, if desired.

YIELD: 7 CUPS

VARIATION:

For those watching their cholesterol, simply omit the cream.

Tomato with Cheddar Cheese, Cream, and Basil

While flipping through the English food magazine, Food Illustrated, *I came across a rave review of a canned cream of tomato soup. The creators, they said, wanted "to create a classic, a dream of a soup." I read their list of ingredients, then came up with my own version (adding a fair amount of fresh basil), and I have to say it is a dream of a soup.*

1 tablespoon unsalted butter
1 Spanish onion, chopped
1 carrot, sliced
2 garlic cloves, sliced
2 28-ounce cans diced tomatoes
4 cups chicken stock
1 cup shredded Cheddar cheese
2 tablespoons balsamic vinegar
½ cup chopped fresh basil leaves, plus additional for garnish
½ cup heavy or light cream (optional)

Place a stockpot over medium high heat and add the butter. When the butter has melted, add the onion, carrot, and garlic, and cook until tender and lightly colored, about 10 to 15 minutes. Add the tomatoes and stock, and bring to a boil. Lower the heat and cook for 30 to 45 minutes. Add the cream, if desired.

Place a small amount in a blender and blend until smooth. Repeat until all the soup has been blended. Transfer to a container, cover, and refrigerate up to three days, or serve immediately, garnished with basil.

YIELD: 8 TO 10 CUPS

Curried Cream of Zucchini

I practically lived on this soup when I first discovered it. Faintly spicy and velvety without being over-rich, it is open to endless variations. It is a perfect way to try different curry powders (or even to make your own), and a great use for assorted vegetables, including cauliflower, broccoli, carrots, or a combination. It is fabulous chilled!

1 tablespoon unsalted butter

1 to 2 medium Spanish onions, coarsely chopped

2 to 3 garlic cloves, pressed or finely chopped

1½ teaspoons curry powder

1 to 2 teaspoons peeled, finely chopped, fresh ginger root

3 large zucchini (2 to 2¼ pounds total), sliced

½ cup white rice

6 cups chicken stock

½ cup light or heavy cream

2 tablespoons chopped fresh mint leaves, for garnish (optional)

2 tablespoons chopped fresh basil leaves, for garnish (optional)

Place a heavy-bottomed stockpot over medium heat and, when it is hot, add the butter. When the butter has melted, add the onions, garlic, curry powder, ginger, and zucchini, and cook until tender, 15 to 20 minutes.

Add the rice and stock, raise the heat to high, and bring to a boil. Lower the heat to low and cook, partially covered, for 30 minutes.

Remove the solids and place in a food processor or blender. Process until completely smooth, gradually adding the cooking liquid and cream. Serve immediately, garnished with mint and basil, if desired, or transfer to a container, cover, and refrigerate up to three days.

YIELD: 8 TO 10 CUPS

VARIATION:

Substitute for the zucchini an equal amount of cauliflower, broccoli, or carrots, alone or in combination.

Cilantro-Ginger with Cream

Rich, velvety, and very, very elegant, this soup is a wonderful way to introduce the distinctive flavor of cilantro to your guests. Its richness makes it better for a starter than for a meal.

Never, ever consider using anything other than fresh cilantro; if you can't find it, don't make this soup.

> ❋ CILANTRO IS THE LEAF OF THE CORIANDER PLANT. IT HAS A STRONG FRAGRANCE THAT SOME DESCRIBE AS SWEATY OR SOAPY. IT IS WIDELY USED IN ASIAN, CARIBBEAN, AND LATIN AMERICAN COOKING, AND ITS DISTINCTIVE FLAVOR LENDS ITSELF TO HIGHLY SPICED FOODS.

1 tablespoon unsalted butter
1 Spanish onion, coarsely chopped
1 celery stalk, peeled and coarsely chopped
2 to 3 tablespoons fresh ginger root, peeled and sliced into coins
2 to 3 garlic cloves, sliced
6 cups chicken stock
½ cup chopped fresh cilantro leaves
1 cup heavy cream

Place a heavy-bottomed stockpot over medium heat and, when it is hot, add the butter. When the butter has melted, add the onion, celery, ginger, and garlic and cook until tender and lightly colored, about 10 to 15 minutes.

Add the stock, raise the heat to high, and bring to a boil.

Remove the solids and place in a food processor or blender. Add the cilantro and process until smooth, gradually adding the heavy cream.

Return the puree to the stockpot and cook, uncovered, over very low heat for 30 minutes, stirring frequently. Be *very* careful not to let it boil. Serve immediately.

YIELD: 6 TO 7 CUPS

Creamy Vegetable

"*The most remarkable thing about my mother is that for thirty years she served the family nothing but leftovers. The original meal has never been found,*" Calvin Trillin once wrote.

I have to admit that, when I first made this soup, I used all the little bits of raw vegetables that were in my refrigerator but now I made it purposefully. If you choose to make it with cooked leftovers, be sure to reduce the cooking time. I have chosen these particular vegetables because they are available all year 'round. This is equally good hot or chilled.

---

2 tablespoons unsalted butter

1 Spanish onion, finely chopped

10 cups assorted chopped vegetables (celery, carrots, yellow squash, parsnips, and zucchini are good)

8 cups vegetable or chicken stock

2 teaspoons dried tarragon, or 2 tablespoons chopped fresh

2 teaspoons fresh lemon juice

½ to 1 cup heavy cream

Place a heavy-bottomed stockpot over medium heat and when it is hot, add the butter. When the butter has melted, add the onion, and cook until tender and lightly colored, about 10 to 15 minutes.

Add the vegetables, stock, and tarragon, raise the heat to high, and bring to a boil. Lower the heat to low and cook until the vegetables are tender, about 25 minutes.

Remove the solids and place in a food processor or blender. Process until smooth, gradually adding the cooking liquid, lemon juice, and heavy cream. Serve immediately.

YIELD: 12 TO 13 CUPS

Ginger Carrot with Cream

Glossy, silky, sweet, and just a bit spicy (of course you can reduce or simply omit the ginger), this pureed soup is ideal for both children and adults. In my house, we especially like to pair it with grilled cheese-and-tomato sandwiches.

1 tablespoon unsalted butter
1 Spanish onion, coarsely chopped
2 pounds carrots, peeled, if desired, and sliced
Pinch ground cinnamon
8 cups chicken stock
2 teaspoons peeled, coarsely chopped, fresh ginger root
½ cup heavy cream
Chopped fresh parsley or chives, for garnish

Place a heavy-bottomed stockpot over medium heat and, when it is hot, add the butter. When the butter has melted, add the onion and carrots and cook until tender and lightly colored, about 10 to 15 minutes.

Add the cinnamon, stock, and ginger, raise the heat to high, and bring to a boil. Lower the heat to low, and cook for 30 minutes.

Remove the solids and place in a food processor or blender. Process until completely smooth, gradually adding the cooking liquid and heavy cream. Transfer to a container, cover, and refrigerate up to three days, or serve immediately, garnished with parsley or chives.

YIELD: 10 TO 12 CUPS

VARIATIONS:

Substitute orange or apple juice or buttermilk for the cream.

Chunky Vegetable Soups

These chunky soups are made with the most hardy vegetables and other than one or two exceptions, are best eaten in the fall or winter, paired with crusty bread and, if you're ambitious, a salad and dessert.

Broccoli Cauliflower with Basil and Parmesan

Practically calorie and fat free, this soup tastes wonderfully rich and, while it can be made with either cauliflower or broccoli alone, it is more interesting when they are combined.

Make sure that you do not add the broccoli until the stock has come to a boil.

GROWN PRIMARILY IN THE UNITED STATES AND THE MEDITERRANEAN REGION, **BASIL** IS A MEMBER OF THE MINT FAMILY. FRESH BASIL HAS A SWEET AROMA SIMILAR TO LICORICE, JASMINE, LEMON, AND CLOVES. ITS DISTINCTIVE FLAVOR IS THE KEY ELEMENT IN MANY MEDITERRANEAN DISHES, SUCH AS ITALIAN PESTO AND FRENCH *PISTOU*. THE WORD *BASIL* IS DERIVED FROM THE GREEK *BASILIKOS*, MEANING ROYAL, AS THE HERB WAS ONCE RESERVED SOLELY FOR KINGS.

---

1 tablespoon olive or canola oil
1 Spanish onion, coarsely chopped
6 cups chicken stock
2 cups water
1 potato, unpeeled, diced
½ head broccoli, woody stems discarded, florets chopped
½ head cauliflower, cored and chopped
⅓ cup chopped fresh basil leaves or 2 tablespoons dried
⅓ cup grated Parmesan cheese, plus additional for serving

Place a heavy-bottomed stockpot over medium heat and, when it is hot, add the oil. Add the onion and cook until tender and lightly colored, about 10 to 15 minutes.

Add the stock, water, and potato, raise the heat to high, and bring to a boil.

Add the broccoli and cauliflower. Return the soup to a boil. Lower the heat to low, and cook until the broccoli is tender, about 15 minutes.

continued on next page

Broccoli Cauliflower with Basil and Parmesan (*cont.*)

Remove the solids and place in a blender or food processor, gradually adding the basil, the cooking liquid, and Parmesan cheese. Do not puree; this soup should be chunky. Serve immediately with additional Parmesan cheese.

YIELD: 8 TO 10 CUPS

VARIATIONS:

Replace the basil with ½ bunch fresh dill, and the Parmesan with ½ cup sour cream.

Replace the Parmesan with low-fat or nonfat yogurt or buttermilk.

Broccoli Rabe, Butternut Squash, and Caramelized Onion

A very odd-sounding soup that combines the bitterness of broccoli rabe with the smooth sweetness of butternut squash. It's an unusual medium for the squash, which is most often pureed.

1 tablespoon unsalted butter or olive oil
1 large red onion, chopped
3 to 4 garlic cloves, minced or finely sliced
½ teaspoon sugar
½ to 1 teaspoon crushed red-pepper flakes (optional)
1 medium butternut squash, peeled, seeded, and diced (about 5 cups)
8 cups chicken stock
1 bunch broccoli rabe, stems discarded, leaves and buds chopped
½ to 1 teaspoon freshly squeezed lemon juice
Fresh lemon slices
Crumbled blue cheese, for garnish (optional)

Place a heavy-bottomed stockpot over medium low heat and, when it is hot, add the butter. When the butter has melted, add the onion, garlic, sugar, and red-pepper flakes, if desired, and cook until the onion has caramelized, about 15 to 20 minutes. Add the squash and cook, stirring occasionally, for 10 minutes. Add the stock and cook until it comes to a low boil. Lower the heat and cook until the squash is tender, about 10 to 15 minutes. Add the broccoli rabe and cook until tender, about 10 minutes. Add the lemon juice. Serve immediately, garnished with lemon slices and blue cheese, if desired.

YIELD: 8 TO 10 CUPS

Beets, Beet Greens, and Lentils

*W*hen *I served this spicy, chunky soup to friends Nancy Olin and Steve Steinberg, no matter how hard I explained that it was most definitely not Grandma's borscht, Steve took great pleasure in exclaiming, after every few bites, "Sally, I love your borscht."*

It is not borscht.

Wash, but don't peel, the beets just prior to cooking. Be careful how you cut beets; they stain most surfaces, including your hands!

1 tablespoon olive oil

1 Spanish onion, finely chopped

1 tablespoon finely chopped fresh ginger root

3 garlic cloves, minced

1 carrot, cut in small dice

1 celery stalk, cut in small dice

1 bunch beets (about 3 to 4), well washed and cut in small dice,
    the greens chopped

1 cup lentils, washed and picked over

10 cups chicken stock

½ teaspoon cayenne (optional)

Plain yogurt, for garnish

Fresh mint leaves, for garnish

Place a stockpot over medium heat and, when it is hot, add the oil. Add the onion, ginger, garlic, carrot, and celery and cook until tender and lightly colored, about 10 to 15 minutes.

Add the beets, lentils, stock, and cayenne and cook, partially covered, until the beets and lentils are tender, about 1 to 1½ hours. Transfer to a container, cover, and refrigerate overnight.

Place in a pot and gently reheat. Serve garnished with yogurt and mint.

YIELD: 10 TO 12 CUPS

Savoy Cabbage with Bacon and Cream

A hearty, thick winter soup. Serve it with a very black rye bread and a salad of mixed greens.

¼ pound bacon, finely chopped

1 Spanish onion, finely chopped

2 carrots, peeled and coarsely chopped

¼ cup all-purpose flour

8 cups chicken stock

2 medium potatoes (about ¾ to 1 pound), unpeeled, diced (about 3 cups)

1 Savoy cabbage, shredded

1 tablespoon caraway seeds

½ teaspoon black pepper

1 to 1½ cups heavy cream

Crumbled blue cheese, for garnish (optional)

Place a heavy-bottomed stockpot over medium heat, add the bacon, and cook until golden brown, about 10 minutes. Set the bacon on a paper towel, and discard all but 2 tablespoons of the bacon fat. Set aside. Reheat the stockpot. Add the onion and carrots and cook until tender, about 10 to 15 minutes.

Sprinkle the flour on the vegetables, stirring all the while. Slowly add the stock, stirring constantly; raise the heat to high and bring to a boil.

Lower the heat to low, add the potatoes, cabbage, caraway seeds, and pepper, and cook until tender, about 1 hour. Do not let it boil again.

Gradually stir in the heavy cream, lower the heat to very low, and cook until heated through, about 10 minutes. Serve immediately garnished with the reserved bacon and blue cheese, if desired.

YIELD: 15 TO 16 CUPS

Chicory and Rice

Although chicory has an unfair reputation for being somewhat bitter, I do not find it bitter at all. In fact, this soup, which I adore, takes on a sweetness as it cooks.

1 tablespoon olive oil
1 small Spanish onion, chopped
3 to 4 garlic cloves, minced
1 beefsteak tomato, chopped
1 chicory or curly endive, very coarsely chopped
½ to ¾ cup Arborio rice
8 cups chicken stock
Kosher salt and black pepper, to taste
Grated Parmesan cheese, for garnish

Place a 3-quart pot over medium heat and, when it is hot, add the oil. Add the onion and garlic and cook until tender and lightly colored, about 10 to 15 minutes.

Add the tomato, and cook 5 minutes. Add the chicory and cook, stirring occasionally, until wilted, about 5 to 7 minutes. Add the rice and stock, and bring to a boil. Lower the heat to low and cook until the rice is tender, about 20 minutes. Add salt and pepper. Serve immediately or transfer to a container, cover, and refrigerate overnight.

Place in a pot and gently reheat. Serve garnished with Parmesan cheese.

YIELD: ABOUT 12 CUPS

Mushroom, Barley, and Leek

This is a hearty, rich, and meaty (but meatless) soup that can be served as a meal in itself. Just add cheese, dark crusty bread, and, for dessert, something sinful.

1 bunch leeks (about 1 pound, or 3 large)
1 tablespoon olive or canola oil
4 garlic cloves, pressed or finely chopped
1 carrot, peeled, halved lengthwise, and sliced
8 to 10 cups beef or chicken stock
2 teaspoons dried thyme, or 2 tablespoons chopped fresh
½ cup barley
1½ cups dry red wine
¾ to 1 pound mushrooms, sliced

Cut off the root end and 3 inches of green part of leeks and discard. Quarter leeks lengthwise and thinly slice. Soak them in several changes of water, being careful to get rid of all the sand.

Place a heavy-bottomed stockpot over medium heat and, when it is hot, add the oil. Add the leeks and garlic and cook until the leeks have wilted, about 10 to 15 minutes.

Add the remaining ingredients, raise the heat to high, and bring to a boil. Lower the heat to low and cook, partially covered, for 3 to 4 hours. (You may need to add additional stock at this point, depending on how thick or thin you want the soup to be.)

Serve immediately, or transfer to a container, cover, and refrigerate. Place in a pot and gently reheat.

YIELD: 8 CUPS

VARIATIONS:

Substitute wild rice for the barley.

Add ¼ cup corn, tomatoes, or spinach when you add the mushrooms.

Fresh Corn with Basil

*M*ake *this straightforward soup in the summer, when corn is at its peak.*

I recently tried to make this with frozen corn. I say "tried" because it was so far from what I intended that I wouldn't even eat it. Don't make it without fresh corn!

1 tablespoon olive or canola oil
1 small onion, coarsely chopped
1 garlic clove, pressed or finely chopped
6 large ears of corn, kernels scraped or cut off (approximately
    4 cups)
5 cups chicken or vegetable stock
Pinch sugar
3 tablespoons chopped fresh basil leaves, plus additional
    for garnish

Place a stockpot over medium heat and, when it is hot, add the oil. Add the onion and garlic and cook until tender and lightly colored, about 10 to 15 minutes.

Raise the heat to medium; add the corn, stock, and sugar; and cook, partially covered, for 25 minutes.

Transfer half the solids to a food processor or blender, add the basil, and puree. Return the puree to the soup and stir to combine. Transfer to a container, cover, and refrigerate up to three days or serve immediately, garnished with basil.

YIELD: 8 TO 8½ CUPS

VARIATIONS:

Substitute fresh cilantro for the basil, and add 1 chopped red bell pepper when you add the corn.

Five Fresh and Dried Peppers

I don't like the taste or the texture of cooked bell peppers except in, yes, you guessed it, soup. Here, since the peppers don't become completely smooth, this soup has a wonderful texture and look that is confetti-like.

PAPRIKA IS A POWDER MADE BY GRINDING AROMATIC, SWEET, RED-PEPPER PODS. THE FLAVOR OF PAPRIKA CAN RANGE FROM MILD TO PUNGENT AND HOT, THE COLOR FROM BRIGHT ORANGE RED TO DEEP BLOOD RED. MOST COMMERCIAL PAPRIKA COMES FROM SPAIN, SOUTH AMERICA, CALIFORNIA, AND HUNGARY. IN THE UNITED STATES, PAPRIKA IS MOST OFTEN USED TO CREATE A FAUX OVEN-BROWNED LOOK, YET IT ALSO HAS A SUBTLE YET POTENT FLAVOR THAT IS A NECESSARY INGREDIENT IN MANY LATIN CUISINES.

---

1 tablespoon unsalted butter
1 Spanish onion, coarsely chopped
2 red bell peppers, cored and cut into wide strips
2 green bell peppers, cored and cut into wide strips
2 yellow bell peppers, cored and cut into wide strips
6 cups vegetable or chicken stock
½ teaspoon Hungarian paprika, hot or sweet
1 to 2 teaspoons Dijon mustard
1 cup sour cream or plain yogurt
¼ cup chopped fresh dill
Freshly ground black pepper, to taste

Place a heavy-bottomed stockpot over medium heat and, when it is hot, add the butter. When the butter has melted, add the onion and peppers and cook until tender, about 10 to 15 minutes.

Add the stock, paprika, and mustard, raise the heat to high, and bring to a boil.

Transfer the peppers to the bowl of a food processor fitted with a steel

continued on next page

Five Fresh and Dried Peppers (*cont.*)

blade and pulse until they are bite size. Return them to the soup pot, and simmer for 10 minutes.

Gently add the sour cream, chopped dill, and ground pepper, stirring constantly. Serve immediately.

YIELD: 8 TO 10 CUPS

VARIATIONS:

Use peppers of one color.

Substitute 2 chopped tomatoes for the 2 red peppers.

Substitute fresh cilantro for the dill.

Broccoli Rabe and Orzo

Broccoli rabe, *also called* rapini, broccoli di rape, *or* broccoli rape, *is not actually broccoli, but another member of the cabbage family. It has a rather strong, almost bitter, flavor and leafy green stalks and tiny broccoli-like florets scattered throughout. I've been known to eat this right out of the soup pot, when it's barely done, and right out of the refrigerator, when it's icy cold.*

 Not a rice, as many people erroneously believe, **ORZO** is a rice-shaped pasta, commonly used in Greek cooking.

1 tablespoon olive oil
1 Spanish onion, finely chopped
3 garlic cloves, pressed or finely chopped
1 bunch broccoli rabe, woody stems discarded, leaves coarsely chopped, and rinsed in very hot water
6 cups chicken stock
½ cup rice, orzo, or any very small pasta
Grated Parmesan cheese or crumbled Gorgonzola cheese

Place a stockpot over medium heat and, when it is hot, add the oil. Add the onion and garlic, and cook until tender and lightly colored, about 10 to 15 minutes.

Add just-washed (but not dried) broccoli rabe, cover, and sauté for 10 minutes.

Add the stock, raise the heat to high, and bring to a boil. Add the rice or orzo, lower the heat to medium low, and simmer for 20 minutes. Serve immediately, garnished with cheese.

YIELD: 7 TO 8 CUPS

VARIATIONS:

Substitute spinach or romaine for the broccoli rabe.

Spicy Carrot with Mint and Feta Cheese

The combination of carrots, mint, and feta cheese always intrigued me, but a chunky carrot soup never appealed to me, as I prefer mine to be smooth. However, smooth didn't seem the right texture for these flavors. When last night's leftover couscous beckoned I couldn't resist tinkering. I love this soup, but be sure to slightly overcook the carrots. If they are even the slightest bit raw they will ruin your soup.

1 tablespoon oil
1 Spanish onion, thinly sliced
1 celery stalk, chopped
3 to 4 garlic cloves, minced
1 tablespoon finely chopped fresh ginger root
1 pound carrots, quartered lengthwise and cut into rough chunks
4 to 5 cups chicken stock
½ teaspoon crushed red-pepper flakes
½ cup couscous
2 tablespoon chopped fresh mint leaves
2 tablespoons chopped fresh cilantro leaves
Kosher salt and pepper
Crumbled feta cheese, for garnish

Place a stockpot over medium heat and, when it is hot, add the oil. Add the onion, celery, garlic, and ginger and cook until tender, about 10 to 15 minutes.

Raise the heat to medium; add the carrots and cook for 5 minutes. Add the stock and cook, partially covered, until the carrots are very tender, about 25 minutes. Add the red-pepper flakes and couscous, cover, and let stand until the couscous has plumped, about 5 minutes. Stir in the mint and cilantro. Add salt and pepper to taste. Serve garnished with feta cheese.

YIELD: 6 TO 8 CUPS

Broccoli, White Bean, and Basil

Unlike many bean soups, this one is best served immediately. After a short period of time in the refrigerator, broccoli has a tendency to get stinky and gray. In addition, the white beans will thicken the soup too much as it sits.

2 teaspoons olive oil
1 Spanish onion, chopped
3 garlic cloves, chopped
1 carrot, sliced
1 head broccoli, stalks peeled and chopped and florets separated
½ teaspoon kosher salt
¼ teaspoon black pepper
8 cups chicken or vegetable stock
1 to 1½ cups cooked cannellini beans, rinsed
1 teaspoon Dijon mustard
¼ cup chopped fresh basil leaves, plus additional for garnish
1 teaspoon fresh lemon juice
Shaved Parmesan cheese, for garnish

Place a heavy-bottomed stockpot over medium heat and, when it is hot, add the oil. Add the onion, garlic, carrot, broccoli stalks, salt, and pepper and cook for 10 to 15 minutes, stirring occasionally.

Add the stock and beans and bring to a boil. Lower the heat to medium low, and cook until the broccoli stalks are very tender, about 15 to 20 minutes. Add the florets and mustard and cook for 5 minutes.

Off heat, add the basil and lemon juice, and transfer the contents to a blender, in batches. Blend until smooth. Serve immediately, garnished with basil and Parmesan cheese.

YIELD: 12 CUPS

Hunter's Soup

In 1988, Regina Schrambling wrote a piece for the New York Times, *called "Eating to Hunt." This is a variation of her Semi-Classic Hunter Sauce. As soon as I saw the recipe I knew that it would make a great soup, and I was right.*

---

* A MEMBER OF THE MINT FAMILY, **THYME** HAS A SUBTLE, MINTY, MILD, LEMON FLAVOR. GROWN IN SOUTHERN EUROPE AND INDIGENOUS TO THE MEDITERRANEAN, ANCIENT GREEKS CONSIDERED THYME A SYMBOL OF COURAGE AND SACRIFICE; IT HAS BEEN TOUTED AS A REMEDY FOR HANGOVERS, MELANCHOLY, INFERTILITY, AND INDIGESTION.

1 tablespoon unsalted butter
1 Spanish onion, finely chopped
1 shallot, finely chopped
2 garlic cloves, pressed or finely chopped
1 celery stalk, peeled, if desired, and thinly sliced
1 carrot, peeled, halved lengthwise, and thinly sliced
6 cups chicken or beef stock
1 pound mushrooms, cut into eighths
1 16-ounce can whole tomatoes, drained and coarsely chopped
1 cup dry red or white wine
2 tablespoons chopped Italian flat-leaf fresh parsley
½ teaspoon dried rosemary, or 1½ teaspoons chopped fresh
½ teaspoon dried thyme, or 1½ teaspoons chopped fresh

Place a heavy-bottomed stockpot over medium heat and, when it is hot, add the butter. When the butter has melted, add onion, shallot, garlic, celery, and carrot and cook until tender, about 10 to 15 minutes.

Add the stock, mushrooms, tomatoes and their juice, wine, and herbs. Simmer, uncovered, until the soup has reduced by one quarter, about 2 hours.

Serve immediately or transfer to a container, cover, and refrigerate.

YIELD: 10 TO 12 CUPS

To make a delicious sauce for pasta, start with 4 cups stock instead of 6.
This should make 7 to 8 cups of sauce.

Mushroom with Frangelico

I used to receive a bottle of Frangelico every Christmas and, being neither a drinker nor a packrat, I looked for ways to use it in cooking. Heating it wasn't successful, but adding it as a finish creates an incredibly subtle and smooth flavor. This velvety soup is best eaten immediately after it is made.

5 tablespoons unsalted butter

5 tablespoons all-purpose flour

4 to 5 cups chicken stock

1 pound mushrooms, stems trimmed, thinly sliced

⅓ cup Frangelico or other hazelnut liqueur

Place a heavy-bottomed stockpot over medium heat and add the butter. When the butter has melted, slowly whisk in the flour until the mixture resembles mashed potatoes. Continue whisking while adding the stock, until it is incorporated and mixture is smooth.

Add the mushrooms and cook, uncovered, over low heat for 1 hour, stirring occasionally. Do not shorten the cooking time or you will lose the depth of flavor that makes this soup so special.

Remove half the solids and place in a food processor or blender. Process until smooth, gradually adding 1 cup stock. Return puree to remaining soup and add the Frangelico.

Serve immediately or transfer to a container, cover, and refrigerate.

YIELD: 6 TO 7 CUPS

Not French Onion

French onion soup is hard to improve upon. While this is a slight departure from the classic recipe, it is as traditional as it comes. It also makes a wonderfully rich stock to use in other soups, especially vegetable soups.

¼ cup unsalted butter

3 large Spanish onions, finely sliced or chopped (about 6 to 7 cups)

3 garlic cloves, pressed or finely chopped

½ teaspoon sugar

7 cups beef or chicken stock

1 cup dry red wine

1 teaspoon dried thyme, or 1 tablespoon chopped fresh

¼ cup Cognac

Place a heavy-bottomed stockpot over low heat and, when it is hot, add the butter. When the butter has melted, add the onions, garlic, and sugar and cook, covered, over low heat for 45 minutes. Stir occasionally.

Add the stock, wine, and thyme; stir, raise the heat to high, and bring to a boil. Lower the heat to low and cook, uncovered, for 1 hour.

If you want a clear broth, pour through a strainer and add the Cognac. If not, just add the Cognac. Serve immediately, or transfer to a container, cover, and refrigerate up to three days.

YIELD: 9 TO 10 CUPS

French Onion

*W*hen I was in high school, my friends and I went to a restaurant that served French onion soup: We thought it was unbearably sophisticated and exotic, certainly something our mothers neither could, nor would, make. Now I know that it is none of those things; it is uncomplicated, speedy, and almost effortless.

Broiling is likely to ruin fine china, so be sure to use ovensafe crocks, with handles, if possible.

---

2 tablespoons unsalted butter
2 Spanish onions, thinly sliced
2 red onions, thinly sliced
1 teaspoon kosher salt
1 tablespoon sugar
6 cups chicken stock
2 cups beef stock
¼ cup dry red wine
2 sprigs fresh parsley
1 sprig fresh thyme
1 bay leaf
1 tablespoon balsamic vinegar (optional)
Freshly ground black pepper
1 baguette, cut on the bias into ¾-inch slices
Thinly sliced Gruyere cheese
Finely grated Asiago or Parmesan cheese, about ¾ cup

Place a stockpot over medium heat and add the butter. When the butter has melted, add the onions, salt, and sugar and cook, stirring frequently, until the onions are very, very tender, about 30 to 35 minutes.

Add the stocks, red wine, parsley, thyme, and bay leaf, bring to a low boil, and cook for 20 minutes. Add the balsamic vinegar, if desired, and salt and pepper to taste. Discard the herbs. Serve immediately or transfer to a container, cover, and refrigerate up to 2 days.

Preheat the broiler and adjust the rack about ⅔ of the way up.

Set serving bowls on a baking sheet and fill each with about 1½ cups of soup. Top each bowl with slices of bread. Top the bread with the Gruyere, then sprinkle with the Asiago cheese. Place under the broiler and broil until well browned and bubbly, about 3 to 5 minutes. Serve immediately.

YIELD: ABOUT 10 CUPS

Roasted Winter Borscht

It's not essential to roast the beets, but it gives the soup a depth of flavor that only roasting can provide. The soup's color is a deep magenta, which almost makes it not look like food.

CRÈME FRAÎCHE IS THICK AND CREAMY, WITH A SHARP, TANGY FLAVOR. WHILE CRÈME FRAÎCHE IS AVAILABLE FOR PURCHASE IN MANY GOURMET STORES, IT IS VERY SIMPLE TO MAKE: COMBINE 1 CUP WHIPPING CREAM AND 2 TABLESPOONS BUTTERMILK IN A GLASS CONTAINER. COVER AND LET STAND AT ROOM TEMPERATURE UNTIL VERY THICK, ABOUT 8 TO 24 HOURS. STIR WELL, COVER, AND REFRIGERATE UP TO TEN DAYS.

---

2 bunches beets (about 8), quartered
4 teaspoons olive oil
1 Spanish onion, chopped
1 carrot, sliced
1 celery stalk, sliced
1 tomato (any kind is fine), cored and diced
8 cups chicken or vegetable stock
¼ teaspoon sugar
½ cup orange juice
1 cup buttermilk (optional)
2 tablespoons chopped fresh dill or mint
Crème fraîche, sour cream, or plain yogurt, for garnish

Preheat the oven to 400 degrees. Rub the beets lightly with 2 teaspoons oil, place on a tray or a rack, and roast for 30 to 40 minutes.

After the beets have been in the oven for 20 minutes, place a stockpot over medium heat and, when it is hot, add the remaining 2 teaspoons oil. Add the onion, carrot, and celery, and cook until tender, about 10 to 15 minutes. Add the beets, tomato, stock, sugar, and orange juice. Raise the heat to high and bring to a boil. Lower the heat to low and cook until the beets are very tender, about 10 minutes.

Off heat, gradually add the buttermilk, if desired. Transfer to a blender in batches and blend until smooth. Serve garnished with chopped fresh dill or mint and sour cream, if desired, or transfer to a container, cover, and refrigerate overnight.

YIELD: ABOUT 9 TO 10 CUPS

Pappa al Pomodoro

*A*lthough I loved eating it at restaurants, when I first made pappa al pomodoro, I thought it was totally bizarre. It is, after all, basically a tomato-and-bread pudding. I tried to keep to the classic version, but ended up reducing the amount of bread by half simply because I prefer it that way; if you find my version not bready enough, double the bread. Unless you are already a fan, you might have to get over a certain queasiness to make this totally delicious but strange-sounding concoction.

Don't use sourdough bread: Use Italian or French.

2 tablespoons olive oil

1 red onion, chopped

4 garlic cloves, finely chopped

8 cups fresh or canned diced tomatoes (about 10)

2 cups chicken stock

4 slices stale Italian or French bread, cut into 1-inch cubes
    (about 3 cups)

½ cup chopped fresh basil leaves, plus additional for garnish

Place a large skillet over medium heat and, when it is hot, add the oil. Add the onion and garlic and cook until tender, about 10 to 15 minutes. Raise the heat to high, add the tomatoes, stock, and bread, and bring to a low boil. Lower the heat to low and cook until the tomatoes are a deep orange red, and the bread begins to fall apart, about 15 minutes. Add the basil and stir to combine. Serve immediately garnished with basil or transfer to a container, cover, and refrigerate overnight.

YIELD: ABOUT 9 TO 10 CUPS

Mushroom and Sausage

Hearty and meaty, this soup is perfect winter fare.

2 sweet Italian sausages, casing removed
1 Spanish onion, chopped
1 celery stalk, chopped
1 carrot, sliced
½ teaspoon dried Greek oregano
1 pound button mushrooms
¼ pound shiitake mushrooms
2 small red new potatoes, sliced
1 teaspoon dried fennel seed
7 cups chicken stock
1 teaspoon Dijon mustard
¼ teaspoon black pepper
2 scallions, julienned

Place a large stockpot over a medium low heat and, when it is hot, add the sausage. Cook for 3 minutes, all the while breaking up the sausage with the back of a wooden spoon. Add the onion, celery, carrot, and oregano and cook for 10 to 15 minutes.

Add the mushrooms and cook for 5 minutes.

Add the potatoes, fennel, and stock, raise the heat to high, and bring to

continued on next page

Mushroom and Sausage (*cont.*)

a boil. Lower the heat to low and cook until the potatoes are tender, about 20 minutes. Off heat, add the mustard and black pepper, and transfer the mixture to a blender in batches. Blend until smooth.

Serve immediately, garnished with the scallions, or transfer to a container, cover, and refrigerate overnight.

YIELD: ABOUT 12 CUPS

Tomato with Goat Cheese

Creamy and rich, yet sharper than a traditional cream-of-tomato soup. Serve either hot or cold. If you reduce the stock to three cups, it makes a great sauce for shrimp and/or pasta.

1 bunch leeks, including greens
1 tablespoon unsalted butter
2 16-ounce cans Italian plum tomatoes, coarsely chopped
5½ cups chicken or vegetable stock
3 tablespoons chopped fresh basil leaves, plus additional for garnish
½ pound goat cheese
Freshly ground black pepper

Cut off the root end and 4 inches of greens of leeks and discard. Quarter them lengthwise and thinly slice. Soak them in several changes of water, being careful to get rid of all sand. Chop well.

Place a heavy-bottomed stockpot over medium heat and, when it is hot, add the butter. When the butter has melted, add the leeks and cook until they have wilted, 10 to 15 minutes.

Add the tomatoes and their juice, stock, and basil, raise the heat to high, and bring to a boil. Lower the heat to low and cook, uncovered, 1½ hours.

Off heat and gradually stir in the goat cheese and pepper. Serve immediately, garnished with basil, or transfer to a container, cover, and refrigerate overnight.

YIELD: 8 CUPS

Todd English's Roasted Vegetable

This is a variation on a recipe that appears in The Figs Table *(Simon & Schuster, 1998) by Todd and myself.*

2 tablespoons olive oil
4 carrots, halved lengthwise
1 large red onion, chopped
1 head Savoy cabbage, cored and cut into eighths
4 beefsteak tomatoes
1 teaspoon kosher salt
½ teaspoon black pepper
2 garlic cloves, minced or chopped
2 celery stalks, chopped
8 to 10 cups chicken stock
2 cups cooked white cannellini beans, rinsed and drained (optional)
1 bunch leaf spinach, well washed and chopped (optional)
Grated Parmesan cheese, for garnish

Preheat the oven to 400 degrees.

Place 1 tablespoon oil, the carrots, onion, cabbage, and tomatoes in a baking pan and toss well. Sprinkle with the salt and pepper. Place in the oven and roast until all the vegetables are lightly browned, about 30 to 45 minutes. Check for doneness and remove any vegetables that are browned. Do not allow any vegetables to burn.

Place a stockpot over medium heat and, when it is hot, add the remaining 1 tablespoon oil. Add the garlic and celery and cook, stirring, until they are golden, about 3 minutes. When the vegetables are ready, coarsely chop them, and add to the pot. Add the stock and beans, if desired, raise the heat to high, and bring to a low boil. Lower the heat to low and cook until the soup begins to come together, about 35 to 45 minutes. Add the spinach, if desired, and cook until heated through, about 3 minutes.

Serve garnished with Parmesan cheese.

YIELD: 12 TO 14 CUPS

Caldo Verde (Portuguese Kale and *Chorizo*)

*T*his *classic Portuguese soup is usually made entirely with water (I prefer half chicken stock), potatoes cooked so long that they are almost mashed (I prefer more texture),* chorizo *served either separately or at the end, and a kind of cabbage not available in the United States. I have mixed it up a bit but the essence remains the same. I have stayed true to tradition only with the kale: It should be cut in very thin strips. Roll each leaf so that it forms a cylinder, then cut through to form ribbon-like strips.*

When you look at the ingredients of this rich and garlicky soup it's hard to imagine that it tastes as good as it does. In fact, before I cooked it I looked at just about every existing recipe to make sure that I had it right. (It is true that some recipes use garlic, some onions, and some other vegetables, but most leave them all out: The result is an absolutely wonderful soup.) It improves overnight so have patience; the wait is worth it.

---

8 to 10 ounces *chorizo,* diced or halved lengthwise and sliced
2 to 3 garlic cloves, chopped
1½ to 2 pounds red potatoes, diced
4 cups water
4 cups chicken stock
½ bunch kale, thick stems discarded, leaves very thinly sliced
  (about 4 to 5 cups)

Place a stockpot over medium heat and, when it is hot, add the chorizo and cook for 5 minutes. Add the garlic and cook for 2 minutes. Add the potatoes, water, and stock, raise the heat to high, and bring to a boil. Lower the heat to medium, and cook until the potatoes fall apart, about 25 minutes. Add the kale and cook for 5 minutes. Using a whisk, gently mash down half the potatoes, to break them into smaller chunks.

Serve immediately, or transfer to a container, cover, and refrigerate up to 2 days.

YIELD: ABOUT 10 CUPS

Minestrone, Ribollita, and Other Bean Soups

When I was in college, I cooked lentil soup all the time, and when I opened my store, From the Night Kitchen, I had not gone much farther into soup making. The great thing about lentil soup was that, while it took what seemed like forever to cook, it more than made up for it by improving with age, being incredibly inexpensive, easy to assemble, and freezer friendly. As I expanded my repertoire, I realized that this was essentially true of all bean soups.

Beans are high in protein, have zero cholesterol, and are an important source of folate, zinc, iron, and calcium. Eat up!

With the exception of the lentil and split-pea soups, all of the recipes in this book require presoaked beans. Unless you have a favored method, here is what I recommend:

1. Soak the beans overnight to prevent the bean skins from popping.

2. In the morning, or just prior to making your soup, cover the beans with water and bring to a boil. Let boil for 5 minutes, then lower the heat to low and cook until the beans are tender.

3. Drain off the cooking liquid (it is the liquid and not the beans themselves that can cause intestinal problems).

★ Salt toughens beans, radically increases cooking time, and decreases quality. Always soak and soften in unsalted water and cook with low-salt stocks.

★ Bean soups cook slowly, and must never be rushed.

★ Feel free to substitute other kinds of beans, particularly in the chili recipes. Unusual beans are constantly showing up on supermarket shelves, particularly in health and gourmet food stores.

★ Although I generally prefer using dried beans because they taste fresher, I make an exception in the case of dark red kidney beans, which I prefer canned.

★ 1 15-ounce can of beans = 1¾ cups
  1 pound (about 2 to 2½ cups) dry beans = about 5 to 6 cups cooked

Fennel *Minestrone*

*L*icorice-y from both the sausage and the fennel, this combination is wonderfully soothing.

2 teaspoons olive oil

1 pound sweet or Italian spicy sausage, removed from casings and crumbled (optional)

1 Spanish onion, chopped, or 1 bunch leeks, washed and cut in small dice

1 large fennel bulb, cored and diced, including the fern-like tops

4 garlic cloves, minced

1 large or 2 small carrots, cut in small dice

1 teaspoon dried fennel seeds

6 to 8 cups low-salt chicken stock

2 cups fresh or canned diced tomatoes

2 cups cooked white canellini beans

2 to 4 tablespoons chopped fresh basil leaves

2 lemons, cut into eighths

Place a stockpot over medium heat and, when it is hot, add the oil. Add the sausage, if desired, and cook for 3 minutes, all the while breaking up the sausage with the back of a spoon. Add the onion or leeks, fennel, garlic, carrots, and fennel seeds, and cook until tender, about 10 to 15 minutes. Add the stock, tomatoes, and beans and bring to a low boil. Lower the heat to low, partially cover, and cook for 1 hour. Transfer to a container, cover, and refrigerate at least overnight, and up to two days.

Place in a pot and gently reheat. Stir in the basil, and garnish with lemon wedges.

YIELD: 12 TO 14 CUPS

Ribollita (Tuscan Minestrone)

After my husband, Mark, and I were married, we honeymooned in Italy. We went to Siena and, after searching for a restaurant, settled on a huge, bustling spot in the middle of town. We sat next to another couple, and the man, seeing me eye his dish, offered me a bite. I accepted, trying ribollita for the first time. I have tried hard to recreate that first sensational taste.

I now add broccoli rabe to mine, but only at the table. My kids haven't developed a taste for it. The bitterness is a great contrast to the richness of the ribollita.

---

1 tablespoon olive oil

1 cup chopped pancetta, bacon, or ham

1 large red onion, chopped

4 garlic cloves, thinly sliced

3 carrots, chopped or diced

2 celery stalks, diced

1 turnip, cut in small dice

1 bunch kale, chopped

1 sprig fresh rosemary

1 sprig fresh thyme

2 cups cooked white cannellini beans

2 cups canned diced tomatoes

8 cups low-salt chicken stock

1 loaf Italian bread, very stale or lightly toasted, cut into cubes

1 bunch broccoli rabe (optional), steamed

Chopped fresh basil leaves

Grated Parmesan cheese, for garnish

Place a stockpot over medium heat and, when it is hot, add the oil. Add the pancetta and cook until it is beginning to brown, about 5 minutes. Add the onion, garlic, carrots, and celery and cook until tender, about 10 to 15 minutes. Add the turnip, kale, rosemary, and thyme and cook for 10 min-

continued on next page

Ribollita (Tuscan *Minestrone*) (*cont.*)

utes. Add the beans, tomatoes, and stock. Lower the heat to low and cook, partially covered, about 45 minutes to 1 hour.

Place the bread cubes in the pot and push down, so that they are completely immersed. Transfer to a container, cover, and refrigerate at least overnight, and up to 2 days.

Place the soup in a pot, add the broccoli rabe and basil and gently cook until heated through. Garnish with Parmesan cheese.

YIELD: ABOUT 12 CUPS

Noah Levin's *Minestrone*

*T*his soup was made to honor my friend Noah Levin, who, when I met him, was all of five years old, a formidable critic, and a blossoming gourmet.

2 teaspoons olive or canola oil
2 small onions, finely chopped
2 garlic cloves, pressed or finely chopped
2 celery stalks, peeled and sliced
2 carrots, peeled, quartered lengthwise, and sliced
2 zucchini, quartered lengthwise and sliced
2 yellow squash, quartered lengthwise and sliced
2 large tomatoes, diced
8 cups beef stock
2 cups low-salt chicken stock
2 teaspoons dried basil, or 2 tablespoons chopped fresh
2 small handfuls dried white or kidney beans, about ½ cup
1 Parmesan cheese rind, about 5 inches
2 small handfuls white rice, about ½ cup
Kosher salt and black pepper, to taste
Grated Parmesan cheese, for garnish

Place a stockpot over medium heat and, when it is hot, add the oil. Add the onions, garlic, celery, carrots, zucchini, and yellow squash and cook, covered, until the vegetables are tender, about 10 to 15 minutes.

Add the tomatoes, stocks, basil, beans, and cheese rind, raise the heat to high, and bring to a boil. Lower the heat to low and cook, partially covered, for 1 hour. Add the rice and cook, partially covered, for 1 hour.

Transfer to a container, cover, and refrigerate at least overnight, and up to two days. Remove the Parmesan cheese rind. Place the soup in a pot and gently reheat. Add salt and pepper to taste. Garnish with Parmesan cheese.

YIELD: 12 TO 14 CUPS

Spicy Black Bean

Rich in flavor and soft in texture, black beans, commonly called turtle beans, *are perfect for soup, but making Black Bean Soup can be a project; it is time-consuming and tends to need lots of adjustments, but is well worth it. Every time—and there have been many—that I have tried to speed up the process, I was sorry. It is best to start this earthy, full-bodied soup the day before you want to serve it; two days before is ideal.*

The freshness of the dried spices is crucial; if yours have been in your spice cabinet for years, please throw them out and get replacements! I always try to use low-salt stock for bean soups. Salt toughens the beans and extends the cooking time.

---

1 pound black turtle beans, picked over, soaked overnight, boiled
    for one hour, drained, and rinsed
2 tablespoons olive oil
2 large Spanish onions, finely chopped
6 garlic cloves, pressed or finely chopped
1 to 2 teaspoons ground cumin
1 to 2 teaspoons chili powder
1½ teaspoons dried Greek oregano
½ to 1 teaspoon cayenne pepper
8 cups water or low-salt chicken stock
1 ham hock (optional)
1½ teaspoons brown sugar
Kosher salt
Black pepper (optional)
¼ cup fresh lime juice
Dry Sherry
Chopped fresh cilantro leaves
Sour cream or plain yogurt

Place a heavy-bottomed stockpot over medium heat and, when it is hot, add the oil. Add the onions, garlic, and spices and cook until tender, about 10 to 15 minutes.

Add the beans, water or stock, and ham hock, if desired, and raise the heat to high. Bring to a boil. Lower the heat to low and cook, partially covered, for 2 hours, stirring frequently.

After 2 hours, check to see if you need to add more water. If necessary, add to 2 to 4 more cups, raise the heat to high, and return to a boil. Reduce the heat to low and cook, partially covered, for 2 hours.

If you want a pureed soup, remove the solids and place in a food processor or blender. Process until smooth, gradually adding the cooking liquid. Add the brown sugar and salt and pepper to taste. (Do not be alarmed: This creates a somewhat grayish soup). If you prefer your soup with more texture, simply skip this step. Transfer to a container, cover, and refrigerate at least overnight and up to 3 days.

Place in a pot and gently reheat. Add the lime juice and garnish with Sherry, cilantro, and sour cream.

YIELD: 8 TO 10 CUPS

Black-Eyed Pea with Collard Greens

Black-eyed peas, so named for the black spot in their center, are a favorite of Southern cooks and are often found combined with sautéed greens, pork, and rice. This recipe was inspired by Sally Belk King, a former editor at Bon Appetit *magazine. Sally is Southern. I am Northern; not as patient, and do not have the same fondness for pork. My version, therefore, has both fewer steps and fewer ingredients. Perhaps this makes it an altogether different soup, but it's still a delicious one.*

½ pound black-eyed peas
Water, to cover
2 tablespoons olive or canola oil
1 large Spanish onion, coarsely chopped
1 carrot, peeled and sliced
1 celery stalk, sliced
2 garlic cloves, pressed or finely chopped
8 cups low-salt chicken or vegetable stock
1 cup dry white wine
1 teaspoon dried thyme
¼ teaspoon crushed red-pepper flakes
2 bay leaves
¾ to 1 pound collard greens, chopped
Kosher salt

Place the black-eyed peas in a pot with the water and bring to a boil over high heat. Lower the heat to medium and cook until they begin to soften, about 1 to 2 hours. Drain and rinse.

Place a heavy-bottomed stockpot over medium heat and, when it is hot, add the oil. Add the onion, carrot, celery, and garlic and cook, covered, until the vegetables are tender, about 10 to 15 minutes.

Add the stock, wine, and spices, raise the heat to high, and bring to a boil. Add the beans and lower the heat to medium and cook, partially covered, for 2 hours.

Add the collard greens, stir, and cook for 45 minutes. Add salt to taste, and serve immediately.

YIELD: 8 TO 10 CUPS

You can use equivalent amounts of white beans and kale in place of the black-eyed peas and collard greens for a soup with a Portuguese flavor.

Lentil and Kale

I cook so much lentil soup that I am never in danger of using an old lentil. However, if you're new to this, be sure to buy lentils at a store that sells lots of them: Old lentils tend to get mushy when cooked, and they just don't look or taste as good.

> ❋ KALE HAS A MILDLY BITTER FLAVOR, NOT UNLIKE CABBAGE, AND COMES IN MANY VARIETIES AND COLORS. MOST KALE IS EASILY IDENTIFIED BY FRILLY LEAVES ARRANGED IN A LOOSE BOUQUET FORMATION. IT IS OFTEN RELEGATED TO GARNISHING HAMBURGER PLATES AT DINERS. THE COLOR OF THE LEAVES MOST COMMONLY AVAILABLE IN THE UNITED STATES IS DEEP GREEN, TINGED WITH SHADES OF BLUE OR PURPLE.

1 tablespoon olive or canola oil
1 large Spanish onion, chopped
6 garlic cloves, minced or chopped
2 carrots, diced
1 celery stalk, diced
1½ cups lentils, rinsed and picked over
1 bunch kale, chopped
10 cups low-salt chicken stock
¼ to ½ teaspoon crushed red-pepper flakes (optional)
2 tablespoons chopped fresh basil leaves (optional)
2 tablespoons chopped fresh cilantro leaves (optional)
Juice of 1 lemon or 2 tablespoons balsamic vinegar
Kosher salt and black pepper, to taste
¼ cup crumbed feta or grated Parmesan cheese, or more, to taste

Place a heavy-bottomed stockpot over medium heat and, when it is hot, add the oil. Add the onion, garlic, carrots, and celery and cook, partially covered, until the vegetables are tender, about 15 minutes.

Add the lentils, kale, and stock, raise the heat to high, and bring to a low boil. Lower the heat to medium and cook, partially covered, until the lentils are tender, about 1½ hours.

Transfer to a container, cover, and refrigerate at least overnight, and up to two days.

Place in a pot, add the crushed red-pepper flakes, basil, and cilantro and gently reheat. Add the lemon juice, salt, and pepper. Garnish with feta or Parmesan cheese.

YIELD: ABOUT 14 TO 16 CUPS

Curried Spinach and Lentil

This is a hearty one-dish meal, especially wonderful to come in to after skiing or sledding. Put the soup on the stove in the morning and, after a long and leisurely breakfast, go outside. When the cold becomes too much, your soup will be ready.

1 cup lentils, rinsed and picked over
1 Spanish onion, finely chopped
2 garlic cloves, pressed or finely chopped
2 carrots, peeled and diced
1 celery stalk, sliced
10 to 12 cups low-salt chicken or vegetable stock
1 tablespoon curry powder
1 large potato, diced (about 1½ cups)
1 to 2 bunches flat-leaf spinach, washed, stemmed, and coarsely
    chopped
1 tablespoon red wine vinegar
Kosher salt
Sour cream or plain yogurt, for garnish

Place the lentils, onion, garlic, carrots, celery, 6 cups stock, and curry powder in a stockpot, and bring to a boil over high heat. Lower the heat to medium and cook, partially covered, for 2 hours.

Add the potato, spinach, and 4 cups stock and cook, uncovered, for 2 hours. Add the vinegar and, if necessary, more stock. Add salt to taste.

Transfer to a container, cover, and refrigerate at least overnight, and up to three days. Place in a pot and gently reheat. Garnish with sour cream or yogurt.

YIELD: 10 TO 12 CUPS

White Bean and Vegetable with Garlic and Rosemary

Totally fat free—and you'd never know it.

1 pound (2¼ cups dried) white cannellini beans, soaked
    overnight, quick cooked, and drained
2 to 6 garlic cloves, thinly sliced or minced
1 Spanish onion, coarsely chopped
2 celery stalks, halved lengthwise and sliced
2 carrots, quartered lengthwise and sliced
1 large potato, cubed (1½ cups)
2 teaspoons dried rosemary, or 2 tablespoons chopped fresh, plus
    additional for garnish
16 cups low-salt chicken stock
1 16-ounce can whole, peeled tomatoes, drained and chopped
¼ cup chopped fresh Italian flat-leaf parsley
1 tablespoon fresh lemon juice or red wine vinegar
Kosher salt

Place the beans, garlic, onion, celery, carrots, potato, rosemary, and stock in a heavy-bottomed stockpot, and bring to a boil over high heat. Lower the heat to low and cook, partially covered, until the beans have fallen apart, about 2 hours.

Add the tomatoes and continue to cook until the soup begins to thicken, about 1½ hours. Transfer to a container, cover, and refrigerate at least overnight, and up to 2 days.

Place in a pot, add the parsley, and gently reheat. Add the lemon juice, and garnish with fresh rosemary. Add salt to taste.

YIELD: 14 TO 16 CUPS

VARIATION:

You can halve the amount of white beans to make this a brothier soup.

Lentil Barley

Another soup that originated from whatever ingredients were lying around; this has become my standard lentil soup. It's as satisfying to make as it is to eat.

Using brown rice instead of the more conventional barley adds a welcome, slightly nutty, flavor.

---

1 cup lentils, rinsed and picked over
4 scallions, including greens, sliced
1 carrot, peeled and sliced
2 celery stalks, including leaves, sliced
1 teaspoon dried Greek oregano
¼ cup barley, or white or brown rice
10 to 12 cups low-salt chicken, beef, or vegetable stock
1 16-ounce can whole peeled tomatoes, coarsely chopped
¼ cup dry red wine
Kosher salt and black pepper
Lemon wedges, for garnish
Fresh basil, parsley, or cilantro leaves, for garnish

Place the lentils, scallions, carrot, celery, oregano, barley or rice, and stock in a heavy-bottomed stockpot, and bring to a boil over high heat.

Lower the heat to low and simmer, uncovered, until the soup has thickened and reduced by about one quarter, about 2 hours.

Add the tomatoes and wine, stir, and cook for 1 to 2 hours. Add salt and pepper to taste.

Transfer to a container, cover, and refrigerate at least overnight, and up to three days.

Place in a pot and gently reheat. Garnish with lemon wedges and fresh herbs.

YIELD: 10 TO 12 CUPS

Pasta e Fagioli

Pasta e fagioli *(Italian pasta and beans) is a hearty peasant soup that is made differently depending on the region; southern Italians make it differently from northern Italians, and Italians in America make it yet another way. This is the American-in-America version, a synthesis of them all. Feel free to experiment with different kinds of beans and different shapes of pasta, but don't leave out the rosemary—it is especially wonderful here.*

Serve this with a ham sandwich for a perfect meal.

1 tablespoon olive or safflower oil

¼ pound pancetta or bacon, chopped (optional)

1 Spanish onion, finely chopped

1 garlic clove, pressed or finely chopped

2 celery stalks, sliced

2 carrots, peeled and diced or sliced

1 cup kidney or white cannellini beans

½ cup tomato puree, or 1 tomato, chopped

10 cups low-salt chicken stock

½ cup dry white wine

1 bay leaf

1 teaspoon dried rosemary, or 1 tablespoon chopped fresh

¼ teaspoon dried thyme, or 1 teaspoon chopped fresh

¼ teaspoon dried basil, or 1 teaspoon chopped fresh

¼ to 1 teaspoon crushed red-pepper flakes (optional)

⅓ cup orzo or 1 cup small shaped pasta, such as ditalini

1 tablespoon chopped fresh Italian flat-leaf parsley

Grated Parmesan or Romano cheese, for garnish

Place a stockpot over medium heat and when it is hot, add the oil. Add the pancetta, if desired, and cook until browned. Discard all but 1 tablespoon oil. Add the onion, garlic, celery, and carrots and cook until tender, about 10 to 15 minutes.

Add the beans, tomato, stock, wine, and herbs, raise the heat to high,

continued on next page

Pasta e Fagioli (cont.)

and bring to a boil. Lower the heat to low and cook, partially covered, for 2 hours.

Remove half the vegetables and place in a food processor or blender. Process briefly. Return to soup and bring to a boil.

Add the orzo and parsley, and cook until the orzo is tender, about 20 minutes. Transfer to a container, cover, and refrigerate at least overnight, and up to 2 days.

Place in a pot and gently reheat. Garnish with Parmesan or Romano cheese.

YIELD: 10 TO 12 CUPS

VARIATION:

You may substitute any kind of small pasta for the orzo.

White Bean and Fennel

This creamy and slightly sweet soup, when paired with a loaf of bread and a salad, creates a perfect winter meal.

2 teaspoons olive oil

1 Spanish onion, chopped

2 celery stalks, diced

3 carrots, diced

1 fennel bulb, cored and diced, including the fern-like tops

2 garlic cloves, minced

1 teaspoon dried fennel seeds

4 cups cooked cannellini beans, rinsed

6 to 8 cups low-salt chicken stock

1 tablespoon fresh lemon juice

Shaved Parmesan cheese

Blue cheese, for garnish (optional)

Crumbled bacon, for garnish (optional)

Place a large stockpot over medium heat and, when it is hot, add the oil. Add the onion, celery, carrots, fennel, garlic, and fennel seed and cook until tender, about 10 to 15 minutes. Add the beans and stock and raise the heat to high. Bring to a boil, lower the heat to low, and cook for 2 hours. Transfer to a container, cover, and refrigerate at least overnight, and up to three days.

Place in a pot and gently reheat. Add the lemon juice, and garnish with the fennel tops, Parmesan cheese, and blue cheese and bacon, if desired.

YIELD: ABOUT 10 TO 12 CUPS

Cape Cod Kale

*O*ne summer I visited my friends Donna Levin and Russ Robinson on Cape Cod and was reintroduced to Portuguese Kale Soup. Donna and I spent our days working very hard and very seriously on our tans (obviously, this was before all the warnings of how harmful the sun can be). The fact that we were burning up at night did not prevent us from craving and eating some of this hot-and-spicy soup each and every evening.

Be sure to follow this with ice cream. We always did.

> ✳ **LINGUIÇA** [LIHNG-GWEE-SUH] AND **CHORIZO** [CHO-REEZ-OH] ARE SAUSAGES HEAVILY FLAVORED WITH GARLIC. LINGUIÇA IS PORTUGUESE AND CHORIZO IS SPANISH; THEY ARE SIMILAR IN FLAVOR AND ARE OFTEN USED INTERCHANGEABLY.

1 pound *linguiça,* or ½ pound *linguiça* and ½ pound *chorizo*
  sausages, sliced or diced
1 Spanish onion, finely chopped
7 to 8 garlic cloves, pressed or finely chopped
1 cup lentils, rinsed and picked over, or 2 cups dark-red kidney
  beans, drained and rinsed
1 pound kale, torn apart by hand, stems removed
12 to 14 cups low-salt chicken or beef stock
1 to 2 teaspoons crushed red-pepper flakes
1 cup dry red wine
1 pound potatoes, unpeeled, cubed
Kosher salt

Place the sausages, onion, and garlic in a stockpot over medium heat and cook until the sausages are rendered of fat, and the onion begins to wilt and brown slightly, about 20 minutes. Stir occasionally. Discard all but 1 tablespoon fat.

Add the lentils, kale, 10 cups stock, crushed red-pepper flakes, and wine, raise the heat to high, and bring to a boil. Lower the heat to low and cook, partially covered, for 1 hour.

Add 2 to 4 cups additional stock and potatoes; stir and continue to cook, uncovered, over low heat for 2 hours. Add salt to taste. Transfer to a container, cover, and refrigerate at least overnight, and up to two days.

Place in a pot and gently reheat.

If you are going to freeze all or some of this soup, omit the potatoes. Add them after the soup is fully defrosted: cook over low heat for 1 hour.

YIELD: 10 TO 12 CUPS

VARIATION:

Add one 16-ounce can Italian plum tomatoes when you add the kale.

Split Pea with Lemon

For years, the only split pea soup I made had the double whammy of smoked meat and heavy cream. While that version is somehow both rich and delicate, the cholesterol and calorie conscious complained. What follows is a version somewhat lower in both fat and calories.

2 teaspoons canola or olive oil
1 Spanish onion, finely chopped
½ pound carrots, peeled, quartered lengthwise, and sliced
1 teaspoon dried tarragon, or 1 tablespoon chopped fresh
1 pound split peas, rinsed and picked over
8 to 10 cups low-salt chicken or vegetable stock
2 tablespoons fresh lemon juice
Kosher salt

Place a stockpot over medium heat, and when it is hot, add the oil. Add the onion and cook until tender, about 10 to 15 minutes.

Add the carrots, tarragon, split peas, and 8 cups stock, raise the heat to high, and bring to a boil. Lower the heat to low and cook, partially covered, until the peas have fallen apart, about 2 hours. Skim off any foam that forms.

After 1 hour, check to see if more stock is needed. If so, add 2 cups.

Add the lemon juice and salt, to taste. Serve immediately.

YIELD: 10 CUPS

★ Note: If you serve this soup on the following day, you will need to add more stock, as the soup will thicken overnight.

Black Bean with Vegetables and Ham

Chunky and spicy, this soup is the result of an attempt to copy a soup I had at the Harvest Restaurant in Cambridge about twenty years ago. When I ordered the soup I expected something smooth, because I'd only had black beans cooked so long they fell apart. I was unexpectedly delighted by this rendition.

Try it with white beans, too.

1½ to 2 cups black turtle beans, soaked overnight, boiled for 1
    hour, drained, and rinsed
2 tablespoons olive or canola oil
1 large Spanish onion, coarsely chopped
1 large or 2 small carrots, peeled and sliced
1 celery stalk, including leaves, sliced
1 small zucchini, coarsely chopped
4 garlic cloves, pressed or finely chopped
2 teaspoons dried thyme
2 to 3 teaspoons chili powder
1 teaspoon dried Greek oregano
1 teaspoon crushed red-pepper flakes
12 cups low-salt chicken stock
2 cups coarsely chopped canned or fresh tomatoes
¼ pound smoked ham, sliced and chopped
Kosher salt
1 tablespoon red wine vinegar
Chopped Italian flat-leaf parsley, for garnish

Place a stockpot over medium heat and when it is hot, add the oil. Add the onion, carrots, celery, zucchini, garlic, and spices and cook, covered, until the vegetables are tender, about 10 to 15 minutes.

Add the beans, stock, and tomatoes, raise the heat to high and bring to a boil. Lower the heat to medium and cook, uncovered, until the beans are tender, about 1½ hours.

continued on next page

Black Bean with Vegetables and Ham (*cont.*)

Add the ham and stir to combine. Add salt to taste. Transfer to a container, cover, and refrigerate at least overnight, and up to two days.

Place in a pot and gently reheat over medium-low heat. Add the vinegar and garnish with parsley.

Y<small>IELD</small>: A<small>BOUT</small> 12 <small>CUPS</small>

Gordon Hamersley's Lentil

*F*or *years, my friend Nancy insisted that this was the best version of lentil soup she had ever made and cooked it constantly. Finally, I gave in, and it is now a familiar part of my repertoire. Gordon says that using distilled water makes the lentils more tender. His surprising suggestion: Empty out the water in your iron.*

> ✳ A COMBINATION OF THE HERBS THAT GROW ABUNDANTLY IN SOUTHWEST FRANCE DURING THE SUMMER, *HERBES DE PROVENCE* USUALLY INCLUDES THYME, OREGANO, MARJORAM, ROSEMARY, AND SAVORY.

6 slices bacon, chopped
1 Spanish onion, chopped
2 garlic cloves, minced
2 carrots, diced
2 tablespoons curry powder
2 teaspoons *herbes de Provence*
3 cups lentils, washed and picked over
10 cups low-salt chicken stock
Kosher salt and black pepper
Grated Asiago cheese, for garnish

Place the bacon in a stockpot over medium heat and cook until it is golden brown, about 5 minutes. Discard all but 2 tablespoons fat. Add the onion, garlic, carrots, curry powder, and *herbes de Provence* and cook until tender, about 10 to 15 minutes. Add the lentils and stock and bring to a boil. Lower the heat to low, and cook until the lentils are almost falling apart, about 2 to 3 hours. Add salt and pepper to taste.

Serve immediately, garnished with Asiago cheese, or transfer to a container, cover, and refrigerate up to three days.

YIELD: ABOUT 10 CUPS

Split Pea with Smoked Turkey and Cream

This is the lightest, most delicate, pea soup I've ever tasted.

1 tablespoon unsalted butter
1 Spanish onion, finely chopped
2 to 3 small potatoes, unpeeled, diced
1 pound (2¼ cups) split peas, rinsed and picked over
1 teaspoon dried thyme
14 cups low-salt chicken stock
¼ pound smoked turkey, chopped or thinly sliced
¾ cup heavy cream
1 tablespoon chopped fresh thyme leaves

Place a stockpot over medium heat and, when it is hot, add the butter. When the butter has melted, add the onion and cook until tender, about 10 to 15 minutes.

Add the potatoes, split peas, dried thyme, and stock, raise the heat to high, and bring to a boil. Add the smoked turkey, lower the heat to low, and cook, partially covered, until the peas have completely fallen apart, about 2 to 2½ hours. Stir occasionally. Skim off any foam that forms.

Add the cream. Serve immediately or transfer to a container, cover, and refrigerate up to three days. Garnish with fresh thyme.

YIELD: 12 TO 14 CUPS

★ Note: This soup can be frozen before adding the cream. Simply defrost, reheat, and add the cream and fresh thyme.

Three Bean

*T*ry *to make this soup with an assortment of beans; in fact, the more the merrier. Although bean soups are considered to be better the second day, this one is great immediately. It also freezes well.*

2 teaspoons olive oil

1 Spanish onion, chopped

2 celery stalks, diced

5 carrots, diced

2 to 3 garlic cloves, chopped

1 teaspoon dried fennel seed

2 bay leaves

6 cups assorted canned beans (kidney, black, white, or fava), rinsed well and drained

8 cups low-salt chicken, beef, or vegetable stock

½ cup rice

1 tablespoon fresh lemon or lime juice

¼ cup chopped fresh basil or cilantro leaves

Place a heavy-bottomed stockpot over medium heat and when it is hot, add the oil. Add the onion, celery, carrots, and garlic and cook until tender, about 10 to 15 minutes.

Add the fennel, bay leaves, beans, and stock and bring to a slow boil. Lower the heat to low and cook 1½ hours. Add the rice and cook until tender, about 20 minutes. Transfer to a container, cover, and refrigerate overnight.

Place in a pot, add the lemon juice, and gently reheat. Garnish with basil or cilantro.

YIELD: ABOUT 12 CUPS

White Bean with Basil

*W*hite *beans are my favorite beans. After they cook for a while, the broth becomes almost sweet, and the beans take on a texture unlike anything else.*

This is a soup for a blustery, cold day; you'll be glad that you made such a big pot.

---

1 tablespoon olive or safflower oil

1 Spanish onion, finely chopped

1 garlic clove, pressed or finely chopped

8 cups low-salt chicken stock

1 tablespoon dried basil, or 1 tablespoon chopped fresh, plus whole fresh leaves for garnish

½ teaspoon dried Greek oregano, or 1½ teaspoons chopped fresh

1 16-ounce can peeled whole tomatoes, chopped

1 pound white cannellini beans, soaked overnight, quick cooked, and drained (page 67)

1 tablespoon red wine vinegar

1 beefsteak tomato, chopped, for garnish

Place a heavy-bottomed stockpot over medium heat and, when it is hot, add the oil. Add the onion and garlic and cook until tender, 10 to 15 minutes.

Add the stock, herbs, canned tomatoes, and beans, raise the heat to high, and bring to a boil. Lower the heat to low and cook, partially covered, until the beans have fallen apart, about 2 to 3 hours. Transfer to a container, cover, and refrigerate up to three days.

Place in a pot, add the vinegar, and gently reheat. Garnish with fresh whole basil leaves and chopped fresh tomatoes.

YIELD: 8 TO 10 CUPS

David Filippetti's Grilled Asparagus Soup with White Beans and Prosciutto

Since few people are going to get out a grill just to make this soup, it's a good idea to plan to make it the day after you'll be grilling other foods, too. Grill the asparagus, then cover and refrigerate until the next day.

¼ pound slab bacon, diced
1 small Spanish onion, chopped
2 garlic cloves, minced or thinly sliced
1 carrot, peeled, if desired, and diced
1 celery stalk, diced
1½ cups diced fresh or canned tomatoes
2 to 4 cups cooked white beans, well rinsed
6 to 8 cups low-salt chicken stock
¾ to 1 pound asparagus, trimmed, grilled and cut into quarters
½ teaspoon black pepper
Shaved Parmesan cheese, for garnish

Place a heavy-bottomed stockpot over medium heat and, when it is hot, add the bacon and cook until golden brown, about 10 minutes. Discard all but 1 tablespoon of the fat. Add the onion, garlic, carrot, and celery and cook, stirring occasionally, until tender, about 10 to 15 minutes.

Add the tomatoes, beans, and stock, and bring to a boil. Lower the heat to low and cook, partially covered, about 1 hour. Add the asparagus and pepper and cook until heated through, about 2 minutes. Serve immediately, garnished with Parmesan cheese.

YIELD: ABOUT 10 CUPS

Chicken Soups

*T*here is really nothing like chicken soup.

I recently made a tour of all the chicken rotisseries and delicatessens in my neighborhood (you'd be amazed at how many that adds up to; after all, Boston isn't New York City), and what I found was that even bad chicken soup isn't that bad.

Some were clearly made from scratch, and some from commercial bases; some were loaded with chunks of chicken and some with vegetables; others were brothy. What I discovered was that people—easygoing, nice people—are generally very, very opinionated about chicken soup.

I have tried to include a variety of chicken soups, taking into account how hard it is to replicate *your* mother's version.

Avgolemono

Avgolemono *is a great soup: It is not only delicious, it is inexpensive, easy, and quick. It has helped me survive many a flu season. Unlike many egg-based soups, this one contains no strips of eggs, which many people prefer. Instead,* avgolemono *is rich, smooth, and almost creamy.*

If you like your avgolemono *thick, cook this a bit longer. If it gets too thick, simply add a little extra stock. If you like your lemon-flavored food very lemony, add some lemon zest.*

8 cups low-salt chicken stock
⅓ cup orzo or long-grain white rice
8 large egg yolks
¼ to ⅓ cup fresh lemon juice
¼ cup fresh chopped Italian flat-leaf parsley, mint, or dill,
    for garnish

Place the stock in a stockpot, and bring to a boil over high heat. Add the orzo, lower the heat to low, and cook until tender, about 15 minutes.

Place the egg yolks and lemon juice in a bowl and whisk together (the mixture tends to turn out a little better if done by hand, rather than in a food processor or blender).

Very gradually, add some of the stock mixture to the lemon mixture, being very careful not to let the eggs curdle. Return the mixture to the pot, and cook over very low heat for 10 minutes. Keep whisking until the stock is combined with the eggs.

Serve immediately, garnished with parsley, mint, or dill.

YIELD: 8 TO 10 CUPS

Carol Lessor's Chicken with Ginger and Dill

Classic Jewish chicken soup.

1 tablespoon olive oil
1 roaster chicken, cut up into parts
1 small onion, finely chopped
1 celery stalk, sliced
1 carrot, peeled and sliced or diced
1 parsnip, peeled and sliced or diced
1 teaspoon peeled, finely chopped fresh ginger root
1 garlic clove, pressed or finely chopped
10 cups chicken stock
1 large potato, peeled and diced, or ¼ cup rice, barley, or small
    pasta (such as alphabet or orzo)
1 to 2 tablespoons chopped fresh dill
Kosher salt and pepper, to taste

Place a heavy-bottomed stockpot over medium heat and, when it is hot, add the oil. Add the chicken and cook until well browned on all sides, about 10 minutes. Set the chicken aside. Add the onion, vegetables, ginger, and garlic and cook, covered, until the vegetables are tender, about 10 to 15 minutes.

Add the stock and reserved chicken, raise the heat to high, and bring to a boil. Lower the heat to low and cook, covered, until the chicken is falling off the bone, about 2 to 2½ hours.

When cool enough to handle, remove and discard the chicken skin and bones. Transfer the soup to a container, cover, and refrigerate at least 4 hours, and up to three days. Skim the fat from the soup.

Place in a pot, add the potato, and bring to a low boil over low heat. Cook until the potato is tender, about 10 to 15 minutes. Add the dill, and salt and pepper to taste. Serve immediately.

YIELD: ABOUT 12 CUPS

Nancy Olin's Chicken

I swear that when Nancy made this stew-like soup for me it had cilantro floating in it, but she insists that it didn't. Still, it's great that way, though not authentic.

1 tablespoon olive or vegetable oil
1 Spanish onion, chopped
3 carrots, chopped
3 celery stalks, chopped
3 parsnips, chopped
1 teaspoon dried Greek oregano
1 teaspoon dried basil
1 teaspoon dried thyme
1 16-ounce can diced tomatoes, drained
10 to 12 cups chicken stock
2 cups water
2 large chicken breasts, trimmed
1 bay leaf
Chopped fresh cilantro leaves, for garnish (optional)

Place a heavy-bottomed stockpot over medium heat and when it is hot, add the oil. Add the onion, carrots, celery, parsnips, and herbs and cook until tender, about 10 to 15 minutes.

Add the tomatoes, stir, and cook 5 minutes. Add the stock, water, chicken, and bay leaf, and bring to a low boil. Lower the heat to low and cook, covered, until the chicken is falling off the bone, about 2 to 2½ hours.

When cool enough to handle, remove and discard the chicken skin and bones, and the bay leaf. Transfer the soup to a container, cover, and refrigerate at least 4 hours and up to three days. Skim the fat from the soup.

Place in a pot and gently reheat. Garnish with cilantro, if desired.

YIELD: ABOUT 12 CUPS

Turkey with Shiitake Mushrooms and Bacon

I only make this soup once a year: the day after Thanksgiving, when I have leftover turkey.

2 bacon strips, chopped
1 Spanish onion, chopped
2 garlic cloves, minced
½ teaspoon dried rosemary
3 carrots, halved lengthwise and thinly sliced
2 celery stalks, halved lengthwise and thinly sliced
½ pound shiitake mushrooms, sliced
6 to 8 cups chicken or turkey stock
2 bay leaves
4 cups cooked and diced turkey
1 teaspoon grated lemon zest

Place a heavy-bottomed stockpot over medium heat, and when it is hot, add the bacon and cook until golden brown, about 10 minutes. Discard all but 1 tablespoon fat. Add the onion, garlic, rosemary, carrots, celery, and mushrooms, and cook until tender, about 10 to 15 minutes.

Add the stock and bay leaves, and bring to a low boil. Lower the heat to low and cook, partially covered, for 1 hour.

Add the turkey and lemon zest and cook until heated through, about 2 to 3 minutes. Serve immediately, or cover and refrigerate up to three days.

YIELD: ABOUT 10 TO 12 CUPS

★ Note: You can enrich this soup by adding 1 to 2 cups cooked white beans, potatoes, pasta, or rice, when you add the turkey.

Chicken with Rosemary

A quick-and-easy rendition of chicken soup that can be made on a weeknight, when time is sometimes short.
If you make this with fresh herbs, add them just before serving.

1 tablespoon unsalted butter or olive oil
1 Spanish onion, finely chopped
2 celery stalks, sliced or diced
2 carrots, peeled and sliced or diced
1 teaspoon dried marjoram, or 1 tablespoon chopped fresh
1 teaspoon dried rosemary, or 1 tablespoon chopped fresh
¼ teaspoon dried thyme, or 1 teaspoon chopped fresh
10 cups chicken stock
½ cup rice or small pasta (such as alphabets or orzo)
1 pound boneless, skinless chicken breasts, diced

Place a heavy-bottomed stockpot over medium heat and, when it is hot, add the butter or oil. When the butter has melted, add the onion, celery, carrots, and herbs and cook until tender, about 10 to 15 minutes.

Add the stock, raise the heat to high, and bring to a boil. Lower the heat to low, and cook, uncovered, for 1 hour.

Add the rice or pasta and cook until tender, about 20 minutes.

Add the chicken, stir, and cook until heated through, about 20 minutes. Serve immediately, or cover, and refrigerate up to three days.

YIELD: 10 TO 12 CUPS

Chicken with Tarragon Cream

This beautiful soup has little flecks of color throughout. It is elegant enough for a wedding or party.

2 tablespoons unsalted butter
1 Spanish onion, coarsely chopped
1 carrot, peeled and sliced
1 celery stalk, including leaves, sliced
1 tomato, quartered and seeded
8 cups chicken stock
1 tablespoon dried tarragon, or 3 tablespoons chopped fresh
1 pound boneless, skinless chicken breasts, cut into strips
1 cup heavy cream

Place a heavy-bottomed stockpot over medium heat and, when it is hot, add the butter. When the butter has melted, add the onion, carrot, and celery, and cook, covered, until the vegetables are tender, about 10 to 15 minutes.

Add the tomato and stock, raise the heat to high, and bring to a boil. Remove the vegetables and place in a food processor or blender. Process until the broth looks like it contains confetti, and return to soup pot.

Lower the heat to medium low, add the tarragon, chicken, and cream, stir, and cook until the chicken is cooked through, about 5 minutes. Serve immediately, or cover and refrigerate up to three days.

YIELD: 8 TO 9 CUPS

Chicken with Lemon Zest, Thyme, and Potatoes

Very light, yet bracing.

1 teaspoon unsalted butter or olive oil
1 small onion, coarsely chopped
3 carrots, halved lengthwise and thinly sliced
2 celery stalks, halved lengthwise and sliced
10 cups chicken stock
1 bay leaf
1 strip lemon zest
1 teaspoon dried thyme
2 medium potatoes, cut in small dice (about 2 cups)
2 to 3 cups shredded or diced cooked chicken

Place a large stockpot over medium heat and, when it is hot, add the butter or oil. When the butter has melted, add the onion, carrots, and celery, and cook until tender, about 10 to 15 minutes. Add the stock, bay leaf, lemon zest, and thyme and cook over low heat for 1 hour.

Place the potatoes in a separate pot, cover with cold water, and bring to a boil over high heat. Cook until the potatoes are tender, about 20 minutes. Drain and reserve.

Add the potatoes and chicken and cook until heated through, about 2 to 3 minutes. Serve immediately, or cover and refrigerate up to two days.

YIELD: ABOUT 12 CUPS

Helen Geller's Matzoh Ball

*M*atzoh Ball soup, though appreciated year 'round, is most often made at home during Passover when Jewish law prohibits eating leavened bread. The consistency of matzoh balls is a hotly debated topic. My feeling is that what you think is best is what your own grandmother made.

This recipe wasn't handed down to me from my grandmother, it was handed down to my friend Donna Levin from her mother and to her mother from her mother, Helen Geller. I am honored to include it here and only wish that I could claim it as my own, or at least as my own grandmother's.

For the soup:

> 1 4-pound chicken, fat removed, cut into serving pieces
> 12 cups water
> 1 teaspoon kosher salt
> 2 Spanish onions, halved
> 1 celery stalk, halved lengthwise
> 1 carrot, peeled and halved
> 1 parsnip, peeled and halved
> Few sprigs parsley
> Few sprigs dill
> Kosher salt and pepper

For the matzoh balls:

> 6 large eggs, separated
> 2 teaspoons kosher salt
> 1 cup plus 2 tablespoons matzoh meal

To prepare the soup: Fill a teapot with water and bring it to a boil. Pour it over the chicken to clean it thoroughly. Repeat twice.

Place the chicken, water, salt, onions, celery, carrot, and parsnip in a stockpot, and bring to a boil over high heat. Lower the heat to medium, and cook for 1½ hours.

Add the parsley and dill, and cook for 30 minutes. Strain, skim off fat, and add salt and pepper to taste.

While the soup is cooking, prepare the matzoh balls: Place the egg whites in a large bowl and beat until stiff. Set aside.

Place the egg yolks and salt in a separate bowl and beat together. Add the matzoh meal and combine with whites. Cover and refrigerate 45 minutes. Divide into 8 to 12 portions and form into balls.

Place a large pot of water over high heat and bring to a boil. Add the chilled matzoh balls, lower the heat, and simmer for 45 minutes. Add to the hot chicken soup. Serve immediately.

YIELD: 10 TO 12 CUPS

★ Note: **This broth makes a perfect chicken stock for use in other soups.**

Mexican *Avgolemono*

I call this Mexican Avgolemono, *because it's made like a classic* Avgolemono *but with Mexican flavors. Serve this as a first course, followed by a peppery, marinated steak and a citrus-and-tomato salad.*

Use a really good quality garlic powder. I rarely use garlic powder, but need it here because there is no sautéing and I don't want any texture.

8 cups chicken stock
½ cup orzo or white rice
½ cup chopped fresh cilantro leaves
8 large egg yolks
½ to 1 teaspoon garlic powder
½ cup fresh lime juice
Pinch cayenne pepper
Chopped fresh cilantro leaves, for garnish (optional)

Place the stock in a stockpot and bring to a rolling boil over high heat. Add the orzo or rice, lower the heat to medium, and cook for 15 minutes.

Place the cilantro, egg yolks, garlic powder, lime juice, and cayenne in a large bowl and blend.

Gradually add some of the hot stock to the egg mixture, then gradually add the mixture to the remaining stock. Serve immediately, garnished with cilantro, if desired.

YIELD: 10 CUPS

Mulligatawny

Mulligatawny is a hearty, slightly sweet, mildly curry-flavored soup. The name comes from the Indian word mulegoothani, *meaning "pepper water," indicating that the soup should be quite spicy. As soup, it had no history in India before the British arrived; legend has it that it was simply an invention to satisfy British army officers who demanded a soup course at dinner.*

2 tablespoons unsalted butter

1 Spanish onion, chopped

1 tablespoon finely minced ginger root

3 garlic cloves, minced

1 Granny Smith apple, unpeeled, cored, and chopped

1 carrot, peeled, halved lengthwise, and thinly sliced

1 celery stalk, halved lengthwise and thinly sliced

1 to 2 tablespoons curry powder

1 fresh or canned tomato, diced

10 cups chicken stock

¼ cup unsweetened, shredded coconut

1 pound boneless, skinless chicken breasts, diced or shredded

Chopped fresh cilantro leaves, for garnish

Plain yogurt, for garnish (optional)

Place a heavy-bottomed stockpot over medium heat and, when it is hot, add the butter. When the butter has melted, add the onion, ginger, garlic, apple, carrot, celery, and curry and cook until tender, about 10 to 15 minutes.

Add the tomato and stock, raise the heat to high, and bring to a boil. Lower the heat to low and simmer for 1 hour.

Remove half the solids and place in a food processor. Process briefly and return to soup pot.

Add the coconut and chicken, stir, and simmer until chicken is thoroughly cooked, about 15 minutes. Serve immediately or transfer to a container, cover, and refrigerate up to 2 days. Garnish with cilantro and yogurt, if desired.

YIELD: 10 TO 12 CUPS

VARIATION:

Decrease the amount of stock used by ½ cup and add ½ cup light or heavy cream just before serving.

Pattie Sampson's Vegetable with Smoked Turkey, Romaine, and Parmesan

This unusually delicious soup came to me from my then-future mother-in-law. In the first year that I knew Mark, every time he came into my shop he described a strange and intriguing soup made by his mother. After months of promises, he brought in the recipe.

I don't salt this soup at all, because it's full of salty ingredients. If you must add salt, don't add it until you've tasted the finished product.

¼ pound slab bacon, diced

1 Spanish onion, finely chopped, or 4 scallions, chopped

1 garlic clove, pressed or finely chopped

1 carrot, peeled and chopped

1 celery stalk, chopped

1 turnip or parsnip, peeled and chopped

8 Italian plum tomatoes, drained and crushed

4 cups chicken stock

4 cups water

¼ pound smoked turkey breast, cubed or shredded

½ cup tiny pasta pieces (such as orzo or broken spaghetti)

6 romaine lettuce leaves, chopped

Black pepper

½ cup grated Parmesan cheese, for garnish

Place the bacon in a heavy-bottomed stockpot over medium heat and cook until it is golden brown, about 10 minutes. Drain off all but 2 tablespoons of fat. Add the onions, garlic, carrots, celery, and turnips, and cook until tender, about 10 to 15 minutes.

Add the tomatoes, stock, water, and turkey, raise the heat to high, and bring to a boil. Lower the heat to medium and cook for 20 minutes. Add the pasta and romaine and cook until cooked through, about 10 to 15 minutes. Add pepper to taste.

Serve immediately, garnished with Parmesan cheese.

YIELD: ABOUT 10 CUPS

continued on next page

Pattie Simpson's Vegetable with Smoked Turkey, Romaine, and Parmesan (*cont.*)

VARIATIONS:

Substitute chicken or ham for the smoked turkey, and/or spinach for the romaine.

Vietnamese Chicken with Lots of Accompaniments

I often crave this soup, and used to go on treks to find it. It occurred to me one day that there is probably nothing so simple to make. It just doesn't get easier, or tastier.

4 ounces rice noodles

8 cups chicken stock

4 thin slices fresh ginger root

2 garlic cloves, thinly sliced

1 lemongrass stalk, thinly sliced on the bias

2 to 3 tablespoons fish sauce

½ pound chicken breast, poached and shredded

¼ cup chopped fresh cilantro leaves

¼ cup chopped fresh basil leaves

1 cup bean sprouts

Vietnamese chili paste

1 lime, quartered

Place the noodles in a bowl of hot water and let sit until soft, about 20 to 30 minutes.

Place the stock, ginger, garlic, and lemongrass in a stockpot, bring to a boil over high heat, and cook for 20 minutes. Add the fish sauce and cook 5 minutes.

Place the chicken, cilantro, basil leaves, bean sprouts, chili paste, and lime in separate bowls for serving.

Drain the noodles and place a small amount in each bowl. Ladle chicken soup on top of each bowl and allow diners to add whatever accompaniments they choose.

YIELD: ABOUT 10 CUPS

Fish Soup

I have made hundreds and hundreds of pots of soup and yet have probably made fish soup no more than a few dozen times. As a rule, I don't think that soup is a great vehicle for fish or seafood. I prefer it in its whole state.

I do, however, make an exception for both clams and mussels, because they are so small and, while less delicate than other fish, absorb flavors well. I don't include instructions for cleaning and shelling, because I buy them already cleaned and shelled, and suggest you do the same. It seems to me that, the less work involved, the more likely one is to make these soups.

> There are always more fish in the sea,
> not as cute nor as rich but fish nevertheless.
>
> **CHINESE FORTUNE COOKIE WISDOM**

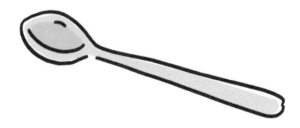

Bouillabaisse

*T*he first time that I made this traditional French fisherman's stew was for a New Year's Eve party several years ago. Since it contains so many different kinds of fish, it's best to make it for an event with lots of people. Serve it for an informal dinner party with baguettes and follow, if you have the room, with a salad. You can also omit the rouille.

Like many local dishes, bouillabaisse's origins and authenticity are hotly debated. Do what they did originally: don't get caught up in the recipe. Buy what is fresh and local.

For the rouille:

> 1 roasted red pepper (page 113)
> 2 garlic cloves
> 1 slice white bread
> 1 tablespoon warm water
> ¼ cup olive oil
> ¼ cup vegetable or canola oil
> ½ teaspoon kosher salt
> ¼ teaspoon cayenne pepper

For the stew:

> 2 tablespoons olive oil
> 2 Spanish onions, chopped
> 4 garlic cloves, minced
> 1 to 2 fennel bulbs, cored and diced
> 3 carrots, chopped
> 2 celery stalks, chopped
> 1 28-ounce can tomatoes, chopped, including the juice
> Zest of ½ orange, cut in thin julienne
> 2 bay leaves
> 1 teaspoon dried thyme
> 2 to 3 teaspoons dried fennel seeds

continued on next page

> 2 cups diced potatoes
> 4 cups chicken stock
> 4 cups fish stock or 2 cups clam juice and 2 cups water
> Pinch saffron, or more, to taste
> 4 tablespoons Pernod, Anisette, or Sambuca liquor
> 1 pound lean fish, such as cod, monkfish, or halibut, cut in big
>   chunks
> 2 pounds mussels, cleaned and debearded
> ½ pound scallops, quartered
> 1 pound shrimp, peeled and deveined
> ¼ cup chopped fresh basil leaves, for garnish
> ¼ cup chopped fresh Italian flat-leaf parsley leaves, for garnish
> 1 tablespoon fresh thyme leaves, for garnish

To prepare the *rouille:* Place the red pepper, garlic, and bread in the bowl of a food processor fitted with a steel blade and process until well chopped. Add the water, and pulse to combine. While the machine is running, gradually add the oils, salt, and cayenne pepper, and mix until thick and well blended. Transfer to a container, cover, and refrigerate up to overnight.

To make the stew: Place a large skillet over medium heat and when it is hot, add the oil. Add the onions, garlic, fennel, carrots, and celery, and cook, stirring occasionally, until tender, about 10 to 15 minutes.

Add the tomatoes, orange zest, bay leaves, thyme, fennel seed, and potatoes, and cook for 5 minutes. Raise the heat to medium high, add the stocks, saffron, and 2 tablespoons Pernod, and cook for 5 minutes. Lower the heat to low, and cook until the stew has come together and reduced somewhat, about 1 hour.

Transfer to a container, cover, and refrigerate overnight.

Place the stew in a pot and gently reheat. Add the fish, mussels, scallops, and shrimp, cover, and cook until the fish is cooked through, about 10 minutes.

Add the remaining 2 tablespoons Pernod, and serve immediately garnished with parsley, basil, thyme leaves, and a big dollop of rouille.

YIELD: SERVES 10

★ Note: How to Roast a Pepper. **Preheat a broiler. Cut the top and bottom off the** pepper. Cut on one side so that the pepper forms a rectangle and place the pepper, skin side up, on a pan about 2 inches below the broiler and broil until the skin is singed. Transfer to a bag and close it. When the peppers are cool enough to handle, peel off and discard the charred skin.

Mussel Chowder

My husband Mark is a mussel fanatic, often going out and buying pounds and pounds of mussels so that he can try lots of different recipes. He thinks nothing of starting with mussel soup, then having a mussel course as an entrée. This one is a great starter.

2 tablespoons unsalted butter

1 Spanish onion, finely chopped

2 tablespoons all-purpose flour

¼ cup dry white wine

1 pound potatoes, unpeeled and cubed

4 cups chicken or fish stock

1 tomato, diced

¼ teaspoon dried thyme, or ¾ teaspoon fresh

½ cup heavy cream

1 pound mussels, debearded and shelled

2 tablespoons chopped fresh Italian flat-leaf parsley leaves, for garnish

Place a stockpot over medium heat and, when it is hot, add the butter. When the butter has melted, add the onion and cook until tender, about 10 to 15 minutes. Slowly sprinkle in the flour, stirring all the time.

Gradually add the wine, and cook for 5 minutes. Add the potatoes, stock, tomato, and thyme, raise the heat to high, and bring to a boil. Lower the heat to low and cook until the potatoes are tender, about 20 minutes.

Add the heavy cream and mussels, and cook until the mussels are cooked through, about 10 minutes. Serve immediately, garnished with parsley.

YIELD: 10 CUPS

New England Clam Chowder

*B*ostonians, particularly Mark and my daughter Lauren, are very particular about their clam chowder and I have to deal with their high standards when I make it. Believe me, it is no easy task.

I desperately tried to leave out the flour but found that it was necessary for the soup's consistency. After much experimentation, I discovered that the tried and true was the best: creamy, full of flavor and comfort.

¼ cup unsalted butter or ½ pound bacon

1 Spanish onion, finely chopped

2 garlic cloves, pressed or finely chopped

¼ cup all-purpose flour

8 cups clam juice, or 4 cups clam juice and 4 cups water

2 to 3 potatoes, unpeeled, diced (about 2 cups)

2 celery stalks, thinly sliced

1 teaspoon dried thyme, or 1 tablespoon fresh

1 cup light or heavy cream

1 pound raw clams, shelled

Chopped fresh Italian flat-leaf parsley leaves, for garnish

If you are using butter: Place a heavy-bottomed stockpot over medium heat and, when it is hot, add the butter.

If you are using bacon: Place a heavy-bottomed stockpot over medium heat and, when it is hot, add the bacon and cook until golden brown, about 10 minutes.

Add the onion and garlic and cook until tender, about 10 to 15 minutes. Gradually add the flour, stirring constantly.

Gradually add the clam juice and, when it is thoroughly incorporated, add the potatoes, celery, and thyme. Raise the heat to high and bring to a boil. Lower the heat to low and cook until the potatoes are tender, about 20 minutes.

continued on next page

New England Clam Chowder (*cont.*)

Slowly add the cream and clams and cook until the clams are cooked throughout, about 5 minutes. Be very careful not to overcook them. Serve immediately, garnished with parsley.

YIELD: 8 TO 10 CUPS

Spicy Clam and Vegetable

Clam chowder devotees find it strange to use clams in a soup other than chowder but, for those who aren't fond of cream soups, this spicy soup is the better option. Serve it with lots of Italian bread for soaking up the last drops.

2 tablespoons olive oil

1 Spanish onion, finely chopped

4 garlic cloves, pressed or finely chopped

1 small zucchini, coarsely chopped

1 large potato, unpeeled, diced (about 1 cup)

½ teaspoon dried Greek oregano, or 1½ teaspoons fresh

½ teaspoon crushed red-pepper flakes

1 cup dry white wine

4 cups water

4 cups clam juice

16 ounces shelled clams, in juice

1 tablespoon chopped fresh Italian flat-leaf parsley leaves, for
garnish

Place a heavy-bottomed stockpot over medium heat and, when it is hot, add the oil. Add the onion and garlic and cook until tender, about 10 to 15 minutes.

Add the zucchini, potato, oregano, crushed red-pepper flakes, wine, water, and clam juice, raise the heat to high, and bring to a boil. Lower the heat to low and cook for 45 minutes.

Add the clams and cook until the clams are cooked through, about 5 minutes. Serve immediately, garnished with parsley.

YIELD: 8 TO 10 CUPS

Chili

Chili is a very controversial dish. Traditionalists insist it should be made only of meat, chilies, garlic, and herbs, but most everyone else has other ideas, myself included.

Beef Chili with Beer

Serve this versatile chili with your choice of chopped fresh cilantro, diced avocados, Cheddar or Monterey Jack cheese, red or yellow bell peppers, sour cream, yogurt, chopped scallions, and chopped green or black olives. Accompany with steamed rice or cornbread (page 178).

1 teaspoon canola oil
1 Spanish onion, chopped
4 to 6 garlic cloves, chopped
3 pounds beef stew meat, cut in 1-inch cubes
1 pound ground beef
2 to 4 tablespoons chili powder
2 tablespoons dried Greek oregano
2 teaspoons ground cumin
1 teaspoon ground cinnamon
1 12-ounce bottle beer (any kind will do)
2 to 3 chipotle chilies (smoked jalapenos) in adobo sauce or
    2 dried chipotle chilies, chopped
1 cup water
1 28-ounce can crushed tomatoes (optional)
1 1-pound can dark red kidney beans, drained and rinsed (optional)
Kosher salt and black pepper, to taste
2 limes, quartered

Place a large skillet over medium-low heat and, when it is hot, add the oil. Add the onion and garlic and cook until golden, about 5 minutes. Add the beef, herbs, and spices, and cook until the beef is coated and well browned. Remove any excess fat from the pan. Add the beer, chipotles, and water, and cook until the beef is tender, about 1 hour. Do not let it boil. If necessary, add salt. If a spicy, beef-only chili is desired, it can be served at this point.

Add the tomatoes and cook for 20 minutes. If a spicy beef chili without beans is desired, it can be served at this point.

continued on next page

Beef Chili with Beer (*cont.*)

Add the kidney beans and cook until the beans have softened a bit, or about 20 to 30 minutes.

Add salt and pepper, to taste. Serve immediately, or transfer to a container, cover, and refrigerate up to two days or freeze up to two months. Serve with lime quarters.

Yield: Serves 8, with leftovers.

★ Notes: If you can't find chipotle chilies, you can substitute jalapeño peppers. You can also substitute additional ground beef for beef cubes. This dish can be frozen.

Black Bean Chili

This is the prettiest chili I've seen. I've always wanted to have a party where I served only black and white food and though I've never quite gotten around to it, I know that this would be a perfect dish, served with a dollop of goat cheese.

---

4 cups black (turtle) beans, soaked overnight
water to cover
¼ cup olive oil
2 Spanish onions, coarsely chopped
4 garlic cloves, pressed or finely chopped
2 tablespoons ground cumin
2 tablespoons dried Greek oregano
2 tablespoons chili powder
2 bay leaves
4 1-pound cans whole tomatoes, in their juice, coarsely chopped
6 to 8 cups water or chicken stock
2 teaspoons kosher salt
Chopped fresh cilantro leaves, for garnish
Goat cheese, sour cream, or yogurt, for garnish

Place the black beans in a pot with water and bring to a boil over high heat. Lower the heat to low, and cook until the beans are almost soft, about 1 hour. Drain and rinse.

Place a stockpot over medium heat and when it is hot, add the oil. Add the onions, garlic, and spices and cook until tender, about 10 to 15 minutes.

Add the tomatoes, water or stock, salt, and beans, raise the heat to high, and bring to a boil. Lower the heat to low and cook, partially covered, for 2 hours.

Serve immediately or transfer to a container, cover, and refrigerate up to two days. Garnish with cilantro and goat cheese.

YIELD: 12 TO 14 CUPS

Chili with Eggplant and Beef

*R*unning *the risk of being biased, I have to say that this Mediterranean-meets-Mexico chili is my favorite. I think it's the combination of beef and cinnamon that I like so much.*

2 tablespoons olive oil

2 Spanish onions, coarsely chopped

3 garlic cloves, pressed or finely chopped

1 1 to 1½-pound eggplant, cubed (4 to 4½ cups)

2 teaspoons dried Greek oregano

2 teaspoons ground cumin

2 to 4 teaspoons chili powder

1 teaspoon ground cinnamon

1 to 2 teaspoons crushed red-pepper flakes

1 to 1½ pounds ground beef

3 to 4 1-pound cans dark red kidney beans, drained and rinsed
    (*see* Notes)

1 28-ounce can whole tomatoes, coarsely cut

1 28-ounce can crushed tomatoes

1 cup dry red wine

Garnishes: sliced scallions, yellow and red peppers, black or Greek
    olives, chopped fresh tomatoes, sour cream, grated Cheddar
    cheese (optional)

Place a heavy-bottomed stockpot over medium heat and, when it is hot, add the oil. Add the onions and garlic and cook until tender, about 10 to 15 minutes. Add the eggplant, oregano, and spices, and cook 5 minutes.

Add the beef, stirring until brown. Add the kidney beans, tomatoes, and wine; stir and cook, covered, for 30 minutes. Remove the lid and cook for another 1 to 2 hours, depending on how thick you want the chili to be. Stir frequently. Adjust spices to taste.

Serve immediately, or transfer to a container, cover, and refrigerate up to two days. Garnish with any combination of sliced scallions, fresh yellow and red peppers, black or Greek olives, chopped fresh tomatoes, sour cream, and Cheddar cheese.

YIELD: 12 TO 16 CUPS

★ Notes: You must use dark red kidney beans: they are the only ones that can stand up to this amount of cooking and still retain their shapes.

It is also very important to use fresh dried spices. If your spices have been sitting in your cabinets for years, throw them out!

Harpoon Chili

*W*hen I met my husband, Mark, he worked for a local microbrewery, Harpoon, and came into my shop to sell me beer. I started buying the beer from him because I wanted to see him as much as possible. Since I really didn't sell much beer, I came up with as many ways as possible to use it, and this chili, into which I dumped bottle after bottle of Harpoon, became so popular it was a constant on the menu.

2 tablespoons olive oil
1 red onion, coarsely chopped
1 Spanish onion, coarsely chopped
4 garlic cloves, pressed or finely chopped
2 to 3 teaspoons chili powder
2 to 3 teaspoons crushed red-pepper flakes
1 to 2 tablespoons ground cumin
1 small (¾ to 1 pound) eggplant, peeled and diced
1 cup dried white or garbanzo beans, soaked overnight and quick
     cooked (page 67), or 2½ to 3 cups canned
1 cup dried black beans, soaked overnight and quick cooked
     (page 67), or 2½ to 3 cups canned
2 1-pound cans dark red kidney beans, drained and rinsed
1 to 2 12-ounce bottles Harpoon ale
1 tablespoon dried Greek oregano
2 20-ounce cans whole tomatoes, coarsely chopped
1 to 1½ pounds skinless, boneless chicken breasts, poached and
     sliced
1 red bell pepper, cored, seeded, and cut into strips
1 green bell pepper, cored, seeded, and cut into strips
Goat cheese, for garnish
Chopped fresh cilantro, for garnish

Place a heavy-bottomed stockpot over medium heat and, when it is hot, add the oil. Add the onions, garlic, and spices and cook until tender, about 10 to 15 minutes.

Add the eggplant and cook, covered, for 15 minutes, stirring occasionally.

Add the beans, Harpoon ale, oregano, and tomatoes and cook, covered, for 30 minutes. Lower the heat to low and cook, partially covered, until the beans are completely soft, about 2 to 3 hours.

Add the chicken and peppers and cook until heated through. Serve immediately or transfer to a container, cover, and refrigerate up to two days. Garnish with goat cheese and cilantro.

YIELD: ABOUT 16 CUPS

★ Note: **If you want to make vegetarian chili, omit the chicken.**

Spicy Sausage Chili

The spice amounts are meant as guidelines; adjust them to your own taste.

---

1 pound spicy Italian sausage, pricked all over with a fork
¼ cup water
1 red onion, coarsely chopped
1 Spanish onion, coarsely chopped
2 to 4 garlic cloves, pressed or finely chopped
2 to 4 teaspoons chili powder
2 to 4 teaspoons crushed red-pepper flakes
1 to 2 tablespoons ground cumin
1 red bell pepper, cored, seeded, and chopped
1 yellow or green bell pepper, cored, seeded, and chopped
2 tablespoons unsweetened cocoa powder
3 16-ounce cans diced tomatoes
2 16-ounce cans dark red kidney beans, drained and rinsed
½ cup dried white beans, soaked overnight and quick cooked
   (page 67)
½ cup dried black beans, soaked overnight and quick cooked
   (page 67)
Garnishes: sour cream, chopped fresh cilantro, grated Cheddar
   cheese, chopped scallions

Place the sausage and water in a stockpot and cook over high heat until it begins to fry in its own fat. Lower the heat to medium, and cook until the sausage browns, about 10 minutes. When it is cool enough to handle, slice it into coins, and set aside. Discard all but 1 tablespoon fat.

Add the onions, garlic, spices, and peppers, and cook until the vegetables are tender, about 10 to 15 minutes. Add the reserved sausage and cocoa, stir, and cook over low heat for 5 minutes. Add the tomatoes and beans and cook, covered, for 2 to 3 hours.

Serve immediately or transfer to a container, cover, and refrigerate up to two days. Garnish with sour cream, chopped fresh cilantro leaves, Cheddar cheese, and chopped scallions.

YIELD: 10 TO 12 CUPS

Stews

Many of the following stews originated as fillings for potpies. I had tired of making chicken potpie, and wanted to try something unusual. While excellent as fillings, I found that each and every one of these recipes could stand alone.

If you want to use any of the stews as a potpie filling, try my favorite topping dough.

> 1½ cups all-purpose white flour
> ¼ teaspoon kosher salt
> ¼ teaspoon sugar
> ¼ teaspoon ground nutmeg
> ½ cup unsalted butter, margarine, or solid shortening, or any
>   combination
> 3 tablespoons ice water

Place the flour, salt, sugar, and nutmeg in a large bowl and toss to combine.

Cut in the butter with 2 knives or a pastry blender, until the mixture resembles coarse cornmeal. Add the ice water, and mix until the dough forms a ball.

Roll out the dough to about ¼-inch thick, to fit top of dish(es). Bake at 350 degrees until the top is golden brown and the filling is heated through.

YIELD: ENOUGH FOR ONE 9-INCH POTPIE

OR 3 TO 4 3-INCH RAMEKINS

Sharon Smith's Beef Carbonnade

*M*any, *many years ago, my friend Sharon Smith returned from a trip to Belgium with news of this dish: a classic Belgian carbonnade, or* carbonnade a la flammande. *She described it perfectly and I set out to reproduce it.*

This recipe calls for dried thyme: Do not substitute powdered thyme; it is much, much stronger and will taste just awful. Also, do not be tempted to taste this in its initial stages, or at least to be prepared to taste the bitterness of the beer. Not to worry; the bitterness cooks out and a wonderful beefy, buttery flavor emerges.

¼ pound bacon, chopped

2½ pounds beef chuck, cut into small cubes, and patted dry with a
   paper towel

2 large Spanish onions, coarsely chopped

1 tablespoon light brown sugar

½ pound turnips, peeled and diced

½ pound carrots, peeled and diced

½ pound potatoes, peeled and diced

1 tablespoon dried thyme

½ cup all-purpose flour

2 12-ounce bottles beer (preferably dark and/or very flavorful)

1 cup beef or chicken stock

¼ cup chopped fresh thyme, for garnish

Place the bacon in a large skillet and cook over medium heat until it is golden brown, about 10 minutes. Drain the bacon and set aside. Raise the heat to high, and heat the bacon fat until very hot. Add the beef, a few pieces at a time, and brown on all sides; set aside.

Lower the heat to medium, add the onions and sugar and cook until the onions have caramelized, about 30 minutes.

Add the vegetables and thyme and cook, covered, for 10 minutes.

Gradually add the flour, stirring constantly. Gradually add the beer and stock. Add the reserved bacon and beef, stir, and cook over low heat until the beef is tender, about 2 hours.

Serve immediately or transfer to a container, cover, and refrigerate up to two days. Garnish with fresh thyme.

YIELD: 12 CUPS

Moroccan Vegetable Stew with Raisins, Herbs, and Rice

A few years ago, Chef's Collaborative and Sunmaid Raisins held a joint contest, asking people to devise a recipe that included both raisins and rice. Except for the obvious, it wasn't such an easy task. Here is my contribution, which took second place:

For the stew:

> 1 tablespoon olive oil
> 1 Spanish onion or 2 leeks, chopped
> 1 tablespoon peeled chopped fresh ginger root
> 3 garlic cloves, thinly sliced
> ½ teaspoon ground cinnamon
> ¼ teaspoon cayenne pepper
> 1 teaspoon curry powder
> 2 to 3 small turnips, diced
> 2 parsnips, diced
> 4 carrots, diced
> 1 butternut squash (about 5 to 6 cups), peeled and diced
> 3 zucchini, diced
> 1 16-ounce can diced tomatoes
> 2 cups cooked chickpeas (page 67)
> 5 to 6 cups chicken stock

For the garnish:

> ¼ cup chopped fresh basil leaves
> ¼ cup chopped fresh cilantro leaves
> Zest of 1 lemon
> ¼ to ⅓ cup goat cheese
> ½ cup raisins or currants

Place a stockpot over medium heat and, when it is hot, add the oil. Add the onion, ginger, garlic, cinnamon, cayenne, and curry and cook until tender, about 10 to 15 minutes. Add the turnips, parsnips, carrots, and squash and, cook, stirring occasionally, for 10 minutes. Add the zucchini, tomatoes, chickpeas, and stock, and bring to a boil. Lower the heat to low and cook, partially covered, until the vegetables are tender, but do not fall apart, about 45 minutes to 1 hour.

Serve immediately, with steamed basmati rice, or transfer to a container, cover, and refrigerate up to two days. Garnish with basil, cilantro, lemon zest, goat cheese, and raisins.

YIELD: ABOUT 14 CUPS

Chicken Fricassee

Fricasee usually refers to chicken stewed in a white sauce, often thickened with cream and egg. I only use cream, which is optional. This is a perfect example of why classic dishes never die.

---

1 fryer chicken, 4 to 4½ pounds, cut into 8 pieces, trimmed of
    excess fat
1½ to 2 pounds any combination of breasts, legs, and thighs,
    trimmed of excess fat
1½ teaspoons kosher salt
1 teaspoon black pepper
1 tablespoon canola, safflower, or olive oil
1 large Spanish onion, sliced
4 garlic cloves, thinly sliced
4 celery stalks, cut in thick julienne
1 pound carrots, cut in thick julienne
1 pound button mushrooms, sliced or chopped
1½ teaspoons dried thyme
2 bay leaves
5 tablespoons all-purpose flour
1 cup dry white vermouth
5 cups chicken stock
2 tablespoons heavy cream (optional)
2 tablespoons fresh lemon juice
2 teaspoons fresh thyme leaves, for garnish
¼ cup chopped fresh Italian flat-leaf parsley leaves, for garnish
Kosher salt and black pepper, to taste

Sprinkle the chicken with the salt and pepper. Place a large nonstick or cast-iron Dutch oven or deep skillet over a medium high heat and, when it is hot, add the chicken, one piece at a time, and cook until well browned, about 3 to 4 minutes per side. This will take two to three batches. Remove the chicken from the pan and set aside. Discard all but 1 tablespoon fat.

Reheat the pan, add the onion and garlic, and cook until tender, about

10 to 15 minutes. Add the celery, carrots, mushrooms, dried thyme, and bay leaves and cook until the carrots begin to soften, about 10 minutes. Sprinkle the flour over the vegetables, one tablespoon at a time, while stirring vigorously.

When the flour has been completely incorporated, gradually add the vermouth and stock and cook until smooth and just thickened, about 3 minutes. Return the chicken to the skillet.

Cook the chicken over the lowest possible heat for 1 to 1½ hours, partially covered, stirring occasionally.

Serve immediately or transfer to a container, cover, and refrigerate up to two days. Just before serving, remove the bay leaves, and add the cream and lemon juice. Garnish with fresh thyme and parsley.

YIELD: 6 TO 8 SERVINGS

Gordon Hamersley's Roasted Vegetable Stew with a Garlic Crumble Crust

Since these vegetables are first roasted, this stew is anything but traditional, but it is hearty and flavorful enough that even the most committed carnivore won't miss the meat.

For the vegetables:

> 2 tablespoons extra-virgin olive oil
>
> 2 tablespoons unsalted butter
>
> 1 red onion, sliced
>
> 1 carrot, peeled and cut into 2-inch rounds
>
> 1 celery root, peeled and cut into 2-inch pieces
>
> 1 butternut squash, peeled and cut into 2-inch pieces
>
> 1 acorn squash, peeled and cut into 2-inch pieces
>
> 2 parsnips, peeled and cut into 2-inch rounds
>
> 1 large portobello mushroom, trimmed and cut into 8 slices
>
> 1 teaspoon kosher salt
>
> ½ teaspoon black pepper
>
> 1 cup white wine
>
> 3 cups water or chicken, vegetable, or mushroom stock
>
> 3 tablespoons tomato paste
>
> 1 tablespoon fresh marjoram leaves

For the garlic crumble crust:

> 2 cups all-purpose flour
>
> 1 teaspoon kosher salt
>
> 1½ teaspoons baking powder
>
> 6 tablespoons cold unsalted butter, cut into small pieces
>
> ⅔ cup heavy cream
>
> 1½ teaspoons minced garlic
>
> Pinch cracked black pepper
>
> ½ cup grated sharp Cheddar cheese

Preheat the oven to 375 degrees. Lightly butter a 9 x 12 inch casserole dish and 2 sheet or roasting pans.

Place the oil, butter, vegetables, salt, and pepper in a large mixing bowl, and toss to combine. Transfer to the sheet or roasting pans and arrange in a single layer. Roast until all vegetables are browned, about 45 minutes. You will need to check every 10 minutes or so to ensure proper doneness; remove vegetables as they brown.

To prepare the garlic crumble crust: Place the flour, salt, and baking powder in the bowl of a food processor fitted with a steel blade and pulse to combine. Add the butter, one piece at a time, and pulse until the mixture resembles corn meal. Add the cream, garlic, and pepper and pulse to combine. Transfer to a medium bowl, add the cheese, and gently mix. Set aside.

When all the vegetables are browned, transfer to the prepared casserole dish, scraping up and including the accumulated bits of caramelized vegetables. Stir in the white wine, water or broth, tomato paste, and marjoram.

Crumble the topping over the vegetables. It should look like the surface of the moon: Bumps and craters are ideal. Transfer to the oven and bake until the topping is browned, about 20 minutes. Serve immediately.

YIELD: 6 TO 8 SERVINGS

Cassoulet, sort of

I had always wanted to try cassoulet. *I thought that it sounded like a great dish, but I hesitated, because it was traditionally made with meats that I couldn't quite stomach. My search ended at Lucky's, a restaurant that used to be in Providence, Rhode Island. On the menu: Winter* Cassoulet *with chicken, sausage, and pork chops, all acceptable to me. I was absolutely amazed. After days and days of exploration, I came up with this recipe, which approximated Lucky's.*

Serve cassoulet *with a salad that has lots of tomatoes in it, and ice-cold beer.*

THIS OLD AND MUCH-DISCUSSED DISH ORIGINATED IN LANGUE-DOC. THE WORD COMES FROM *CASSOLE*, THE NAME OF THE GLAZED EARTHENWARE COOKING POT TRADITIONALLY USED. THERE ARE THREE MAIN TYPES OF **CASSOULET,** DEPENDING ON THE MEAT USED: THE OLDEST, FROM CASTELNAUDARY, CONTAINS PORK; THE SECOND FROM CARCASSONE, WHERE LEG OF MUTTON AND SOMETIMES PARTRIDGE IS USED; AND THE THIRD, FROM TOULOUSE, WHICH USED LARD, TOULOUSE SAUSAGE, MUTTON, AND DUCK OR GOOSE. IN 1966, *THE ETATS GENERAUX DE LA GASTRONOMIE FRANCAISE* DECREED THE FOLLOWING PROPORTIONS FOR *CASSOULET:* AT LEAST 30 PERCENT PORK, MUTTON OR PRESERVED GOOSE, 70 PERCENT HARICOT BEANS AND STOCK, FRESH PORK RINDS, HERBS, AND FLAVORINGS. TODAY, IN THIS COUNTRY, THE NAME HAS COME TO MEAN ANY KIND OF STEW FEATURING BEANS, PORK, AND, OFTEN, DUCK.

½ cup olive oil
½ cup all-purpose flour
2 Spanish onions, finely chopped
6 to 8 garlic cloves, pressed or finely chopped
2 carrots, peeled and diced
2 celery stalks, diced
2 spicy Italian sausages, pricked all over with a fork

¼ cup water

1 pork chop

2 whole chicken breasts, trimmed of excess fat

1½ cups dry red wine

3 to 3½ cups chicken stock

1½ pounds white cannellini beans, soaked overnight

1½ teaspoons ground nutmeg

1½ tablespoons dried thyme, or 4½ tablespoons fresh

2 bay leaves

½ cup chopped fresh Italian flat-leaf parsley

½ cup breadcrumbs

Place a stockpot over high heat and, when it is hot, add the oil. Slowly whisk in the flour. Be very careful when you do this (you may want to stand back at first). Cook over high heat, whisking constantly, until the mixture becomes dark red, almost black, about 20 minutes.

Lower the heat to low and carefully add the onions, garlic, carrots, and celery. The oil will sizzle when you do this. Cook until tender, about 10 to 15 minutes.

Place the sausages and water in a frying pan and cook over high heat until they fry in their own fat. Remove and set aside.

Reheat the pan, add the pork chop, and cook until medium rare, about 10 to 12 minutes. Remove the pork chop, add the chicken, and cook until it is opaque throughout and the juices run clear, 10 to 15 minutes. When they are cool enough to handle, cut the meats into serving pieces (you can make them bite size or leave them whole), and set aside.

Add the wine, stock, beans, and spices to the vegetables, stir, and cook over low heat for 2 hours.

Preheat the oven to 350 degrees.

Place the parsley and breadcrumbs in a small bowl and toss to combine.

Add the reserved meats to the pan, mix to combine, and transfer the entire mixture to an ovenproof casserole. Sprinkle with the parsley mixture, and transfer to the oven. After 30 minutes, the bread crumbs should

continued on next page

Cassoulet, sort of *(cont.)*

have formed a crust. Push this down into the beans. Repeat this step twice; the third time do not push bread crumbs back in but instead leave it as the crust.

Serve immediately.

Y I E L D : S E R V E S 6

Classic Beef Stew

I often make big batches of this hearty, comforting stew in the late fall and winter. I try to make enough for two meals, one to eat and one to freeze. There is nothing better than having something to defrost that usually takes hours and hours to make. Serve this with biscuits (page 181).

2 tablespoons olive oil, or additional bacon or fat

2 large Spanish onions, coarsely chopped

4 garlic cloves, pressed or finely chopped

1 pound celery (about ½ bunch), sliced

1 pound carrots, peeled and sliced

¼ pound bacon, chopped

½ to 1 cup all-purpose flour

1½ teaspoons kosher salt

½ teaspoon black pepper

2½ pounds beef chuck, cut into cubes

2 cups dry red wine

2 cups beef or chicken stock

1 16-ounce can Italian plum tomatoes, coarsely chopped, including the juice

1 tablespoon dried thyme, or 3 tablespoons chopped fresh thyme

2 bay leaves

1½ pounds potatoes, unpeeled, cut into cubes

¼ cup chopped fresh Italian flat-leaf parsley leaves, for garnish

Place a stockpot over medium heat and, when it is hot, add the oil. Add the onions, garlic, celery, and carrots and cook until tender, about 15 minutes.

While the vegetables are sautéing, place the bacon in a large skillet over medium heat. Cook until the fat is rendered, about 5 to 7 minutes. Drain and set aside.

Place the flour, salt, and pepper in a bag and shake to combine. Add the beef cubes and shake until the cubes are finely dusted. Reheat the skillet,

continued on next page

Classic Beef Stew (*cont.*)

and raise the heat to high. Add the beef, one layer at a time, and cook until deeply browned on all sides. You will need to do this in 2 or 3 batches.

As the meat browns, add it to the stockpot. When all the beef has browned, slowly add the wine to the skillet, scraping the bottom, and transfer the mixture to the stockpot.

Slowly add the stock, tomatoes, thyme, and bay leaves and, when it comes to a low boil, lower the heat to low and simmer until the beef is very tender, about 2 hours. Discard the bay leaves.

Boil the potatoes in a separate pot, and add to the stew about 30 minutes before serving or, if you wish, serve them on the side. Garnish with parsley.

YIELD: 12 TO 15 CUPS

Curried Beef Stew

The best beef to use for this lush and spicy stew (and all the others, for that matter) is beef chuck, which is from the neck and shoulder area of the cow. Only tough cuts of meat should be used, because they are able to stand up to the long cooking process. Tender meat, such as tenderloin or sirloin, toughens the longer it cooks; stew meat or chuck will break down and become more tender and more flavorful when cooked for long periods of time.

¼ cup all-purpose flour

¼ cup curry powder

2½ pounds beef chuck, cut into ½-inch cubes, patted dry with a
    paper towel

2 to 4 tablespoons olive oil

1 tablespoon light brown sugar

2 tablespoons ground cumin

2 Spanish onions, coarsely chopped

4 garlic cloves, pressed or finely chopped

2 tablespoons peeled, finely chopped fresh ginger root

1 orange or tangerine, peeled, seeded, and coarsely chopped

1 28-ounce can whole tomatoes, coarsely chopped

Place the flour, curry powder, salt, and pepper in a bag and shake to combine. Add the beef cubes and shake until the cubes are finely dusted.

Place a stockpot over medium-high heat and, when it is hot, add the oil. Add the beef, one layer at a time, and cook until deeply browned on all sides. You will need to do this in 2 or 3 batches. Set aside.

Add the brown sugar, cumin, onions, and garlic to the pot, and cook until the onions have started to caramelize, about 40 minutes. (You may need to add extra oil.)

Add the ginger, orange, and tomatoes. Cook over low heat until the beef is very tender, about 2 to 3 hours. Serve immediately or transfer to a container, cover, and refrigerate overnight.

YIELD: 11 TO 12 CUPS

Curried Chicken Stew

This is a quick-and-easy stew, a faultless dish to serve for unexpected company. It tastes as if you've been slaving over a hot stove all day. Serve it with basmati rice and a green salad.

2 tablespoons olive or safflower oil
2 Spanish onions, coarsely chopped
3 garlic cloves, pressed or finely chopped
1 tablespoon minced fresh ginger root
3 1-pound cans Italian plum tomatoes, coarsely chopped
⅓ cup mango or apple chutney
2 Granny Smith apples, peaches, or mangoes, cored, peeled, and diced
¼ cup curry powder, or more, to taste
3 pounds boneless, skinless chicken breasts, cut into large cubes
4 to 5 cups chicken stock
1 cup frozen peas
4 cups packed bunch or baby spinach
½ cup chopped fresh cilantro leaves, plus additional, for garnish
Kosher salt
Black pepper
Yogurt or crème fraîche, for garnish

Place a heavy-bottomed stockpot over medium heat and when it is hot, add the oil. Add the onions, garlic, and ginger and cook until tender, about 10 to 15 minutes.

Add the tomatoes, chutney, apples, and curry powder and cook for 5 minutes. Add the chicken and cook until it changes color to yellow, about 5 minutes. Add the stock, and cook for 1 hour.

Add the peas, spinach, and cilantro and cook 5 minutes.

Serve immediately or transfer to a container, cover, and refrigerate overnight. Add salt and pepper, to taste. Garnish with fresh cilantro and yogurt or crème fraîche.

YIELD: 12 TO 14 CUPS

Chilled Soups

*I*n the not-so-distant past, only a few soups were considered appropriate for chilling, such as *gazpacho* and *vichyssoise*. However, it is now acceptable to chill almost anything, depending on your taste. I had one customer who ate her chili chilled and another who heated up *gazpacho*!

The recipes in this chapter are almost always served chilled. However, the hot soups listed here are also delicious chilled.

Asparagus with Fresh Herbs
Carrot with Fennel
Ginger Carrot with Cream
Fresh Corn with Basil
Five Fresh and Dried Peppers
Parsnip with Sour Cream and Mustard
Tomato with Goat Cheese
Triple Tomato
Creamy Vegetable
Curried Cream of Zucchini

The following chilled soups may also be served hot. Simply serve them as soon as preparation is completed. They may be reheated *gently;* do not let them boil.

Curried Cream of Fresh Pea

Spinach with Garlic, Lemon, and Yogurt

Vichyssoise

Ginger Melon

*This is terrifically refreshing, perfect for lunch or dinner on a hot sum-
mer day when appetites are flagging. If you want to spice it up, add the
chili pepper of your choice.*

---

1 cantaloupe, peeled, seeded, and chopped
1 honeydew melon, peeled, seeded, and chopped
1½ cups plain yogurt
1½ tablespoons peeled, finely chopped fresh ginger root
¼ teaspoon ground cinnamon
¼ cup lightly toasted walnuts
Chopped fresh mint leaves, for garnish

Place all the ingredients in the bowl of a food processor fitted with a
steel blade, and process until smooth. Transfer to a container, cover, and refrigerate at least 1 hour, and up to 4 hours. Garnish with mint.

YIELD: 7 TO 8 CUPS

Chilled Borscht

Years and years ago, I had a roommate named Amy, who taught me how to make borscht, one of the few soups I had never, ever considered making. I assumed it would be awful but, in Amy's hands, it was creamy and tart and just sublime. Here it is.

2 large bunches beets (about 8 cups), peeled, if desired, and thinly sliced
6 cups water or chicken stock
⅓ cup sugar (optional)
2 tablespoons fresh lemon juice
2 cups yogurt or buttermilk
Kosher salt and black pepper, to taste
1 to 2 tablespoons chopped fresh dill, for garnish
1 pickling cucumber, thinly sliced, for garnish
Yogurt, for garnish (optional)

Place the beets, water or stock, and sugar, if desired, in a heavy-bottomed stockpot and bring to a boil. Lower the heat to low and cook, partially covered, until the beets are tender, about 35 minutes. Set aside to cool to room temperature.

Place the beets in a blender or food processor fitted with a steel blade and process, gradually adding the cooking liquid, lemon juice, and buttermilk, until smooth. If necessary, this can be done in 2 batches. Cover, and refrigerate at least 2 hours.

Add salt and pepper to taste, and garnish with dill, cucumber, and yogurt, if desired.

YIELD: 10 TO 12 CUPS

Tomato Cucumber

A creamy and tart chilled soup from the Mediterranean.

¼ cup fresh lemon juice

1 46-ounce can tomato juice

2 tablespoons corn or safflower oil

1½ tablespoons curry powder

½ cup chopped fresh Italian flat-leaf parsley leaves, plus
    additional, for garnish

¼ cup red wine vinegar

1 cup buttermilk

2 cups plain yogurt

2 cucumbers, peeled, seeded, and finely sliced

Place all the ingredients, except the cucumbers, in a blender or a food processor fitted with a steel blade. Process until smooth. By hand, stir in the cucumbers. Transfer to a container, cover, and refrigerate, at least 1 hour, and up to 4 hours. Garnish with parsley.

YIELD: 9 CUPS

Curried Chicken

Rich, creamy, spicy, and slightly sweet.

1 tablespoon unsalted butter
1 bunch scallions, whites chopped, and greens thinly sliced,
    for garnish
2 garlic cloves, thinly sliced
1 tablespoon peeled chopped fresh ginger root
⅓ cup grated, unsweetened, dried or fresh coconut
2 carrots, peeled, if desired, and sliced
1 celery stalk, sliced
2 to 3 tablespoons curry powder
6 cups chicken stock
¾ to 1 pound skinless, boneless chicken breast
1 cup heavy cream
1 large orange, peeled and chopped, for garnish
3 to 4 tablespoons chopped fresh cilantro leaves, for garnish

Place a stockpot over a medium-high heat and, when it is hot, add the butter. Add the scallion whites, garlic, ginger, coconut, carrot, and celery and cook until the coconut is golden brown, about 5 minutes. Add the curry and cook for 1 minute.

Add the stock and chicken and bring to a boil. Lower the heat to low and cook until the chicken is cooked throughout, about 10 minutes. It is not necessary for the vegetables to be completely cooked. Remove the chicken and, when it is cool enough to handle, chop it.

Place the remaining cooking liquid in a blender, one cup at a time, and blend until smooth, gradually adding the cream. Add the reserved chicken and mix to combine. Transfer to a container, cover, and refrigerate until it is very, very cold, about 4 hours. Garnish with scallion greens, orange, and cilantro.

YIELD: ABOUT 8 TO 10 CUPS

VARIATION:

You can substitute shrimp for the chicken.

Cucumber Walnut

This slightly chunky soup is of Middle Eastern inspiration. Try it before a dinner of broiled chicken or lamb.

1 cup coarsely chopped, toasted walnuts
2 garlic cloves, pressed or finely chopped
2 cups plain yogurt
2 cups buttermilk
1 teaspoon kosher salt
1 teaspoon black pepper
2 English cucumbers, diced
Fresh mint leaves, Italian flat-leaf parsley leaves, or chives,
    for garnish

Place the walnuts, garlic, yogurt, buttermilk, salt, and pepper in the bowl of a food processor fitted with a steel blade and process until smooth.

By hand, stir in the cucumbers. Transfer to a container, cover, and refrigerate at least 2 hours, and up to 4 hours. Garnish with mint, parsley, or chives.

YIELD: 6 CUPS

Cream of Avocado

Buttery and refined, this is an avocado lover's dream come true. All you need to do is fill an espresso cup with this rich, creamy, and absolutely decadent avocado cream.

Like the tomato, avocados are considered a vegetable, but are actually a fruit. My favorite avocado is the buttery, thick-skinned, bumpy almost-black Haas. A ripe avocado will yield slightly when pressed.

When removing the flesh from the skin, cut the avocado in half and twist the two halves away from each other. Pop the pit out, and scoop out the flesh.

---

1 tablespoon unsalted butter

1 very small onion, chopped (about ⅓ cup)

2 teaspoons peeled finely chopped, fresh ginger root

2 to 3 garlic cloves, minced

2 perfectly ripe Haas avocados, halved, pitted, and scooped out

¼ cup fresh basil leaves, plus additional, for garnish

¼ cup fresh cilantro leaves, plus additional, for garnish

¼ to ⅓ cup heavy cream

¼ to ⅓ cup fresh lime juice

3½ cups ice water

Cayenne pepper to taste

Kosher salt and black pepper, to taste

Place a small pan over medium low heat, and when it is hot, add the butter. When the butter has melted, add the onion, ginger, and garlic and cook until golden, about 10 minutes. Set aside to cool for 5 minutes.

Place the avocados, basil, cilantro, cream, and lime juice in a blender and blend until pureed. Gradually, while the machine is running, add the water and reserved onion mixture and blend until completely smooth. Add the cayenne and salt and pepper to taste. Transfer to a container, cover, and refrigerate at least 2 hours and up to overnight. Garnish with basil and cilantro.

YIELD: ABOUT 5 CUPS

Avocado and Shrimp "Seviche"

Unlike a real seviche, which includes raw fish that gets cooked in lemon or lime juice, this one starts with cooked shrimp.

1 pound steamed or grilled shrimp, cut into large chunks
Grated zest and juice of 2 limes
3 tablespoons chopped fresh cilantro leaves
2 perfectly ripe avocados, cubed
½ cup chopped fresh pineapple
1 large tomato, cored and chopped
¼ teaspoon crushed red-pepper flakes
½ teaspoon kosher salt
Tortilla chips

Place the shrimp, lime zest and juice, cilantro, avocado, pineapple, tomato, crushed red-pepper flakes, and salt in a large glass or ceramic bowl and toss to combine.

Transfer to a container, cover, and refrigerate at least 20 minutes, but no longer than 1 hour. Serve with tortilla chips.

YIELD: SERVES 4

Summer *Minestrone*

*T*hough the idea of chilled minestrone *may seem strange, this soup was designed to be chilled; it is not simply a hot minestrone that gets eaten right from the fridge. It utilizes the best vegetables of summer, and is hearty enough to serve as a meal, accompanied by bread. You can also dress it up with steamed or grilled shrimp.*

1 teaspoon olive oil
½ Spanish onion, chopped
2 celery stalks, including leaves, chopped
1 garlic clove, minced
1 cup fresh fava beans, shelled (start with about 1 pound)
3½ cups chicken stock
1 cup fresh peas (start with about 1 pound)
1 pound asparagus, woody stems removed, remainder chopped
1 cup fresh corn kernels (about 1 or 2 ears)
⅔ cup freshly grated Parmesan cheese
⅓ cup heavy cream
1 large beefsteak tomato, chopped
⅓ to ½ cup chopped fresh basil leaves
Kosher salt and black pepper, to taste
Whole basil leaves, for garnish

Place a stockpot over medium heat and, when it is hot, add the oil. Add the onion, celery, and garlic and cook until tender, about 10 to 15 minutes. Add the fava beans and stock and bring to a boil. Lower the heat to low and cook until the beans are soft, about 15 to 20 minutes.

Off heat, add the peas, asparagus, corn, and Parmesan cheese. Stir until the Parmesan has melted. Set aside to cool to room temperature.

Place 1½ cups of the solids in a blender and, while the blender is going, gradually add the cream. Process until smooth and return to the soup pot. (If you want a smooth soup, blend all of it at this point.) Add the tomato, basil, and salt and pepper to taste.

Transfer to a container, cover, and refrigerate at least 2 hours and up to overnight. Garnish with basil leaves.

YIELD: ABOUT 7 TO 8 CUPS

Curried Cream of Fresh Pea

Suave and subtle, this is a great beginning for an elegant dinner. When I first made this, it seemed such a shame to chill it, because it was absolutely delicious hot, too.

2 tablespoons unsalted butter
1 Spanish onion, coarsely chopped
2 garlic cloves, minced
2 tablespoons curry powder
1¼ to 1½ pounds fresh or frozen peas
3½ cups water or chicken stock
½ to 1 cup heavy cream
Pinch freshly ground nutmeg
Kosher salt, to taste
Fresh chives, for garnish

Place a medium saucepan over medium heat and, when it is hot, add the butter. When the butter has melted, add the onion and garlic and cook until tender, about 10 to 15 minutes. Add the curry powder and cook for 3 to 4 minutes, stirring occasionally.

Add the peas and stock, raise the heat to high, and bring to a boil. Lower the heat to low and cook for 35 to 45 minutes.

Place the solids in a food processor or blender. Process until smooth, gradually adding cooking liquid, cream, and nutmeg. Add salt to taste.

Transfer to a container, cover, and refrigerate at least 2 hours and up to overnight. Garnish with chives.

YIELD: 7 TO 8 CUPS

Carol Lessor's Moroccan Tomato Soup

A great and unusual chilled tomato soup given to me by my old running pal, Carol Lessor.

4 to 5 garlic cloves, finely chopped or pressed
1 tablespoon Hungarian paprika
2 to 3 teaspoons ground cumin
8 fresh tomatoes, diced
¼ cup chopped fresh cilantro leaves, plus additional for garnish
¼ cup white vinegar
Kosher salt and black pepper, to taste
Yogurt, for garnish

Place all the ingredients in a bowl and mix to combine. Remove half the mixture and place in the bowl of a food processor fitted with a steel blade and puree. Return to the bowl. Add salt and pepper to taste.

Transfer to a container, cover, and refrigerate at least 2 hours, and up to overnight.

Garnish with cilantro and yogurt.

YIELD: 6 TO 8 CUPS

Spinach with Garlic, Lemon, and Yogurt

Make this soup with flat bunches of spinach instead of the ubiquitous curly version available in plastic bags. It is worth seeking out the more flavorful variety.

2 tablespoons olive oil

8 garlic cloves, pressed or finely chopped

2 bunches flat-leaf spinach, thoroughly washed and coarsely chopped

4 cups chicken stock

2 tablespoons fresh lemon juice

½ cup plain yogurt, cream, or sour cream

Kosher salt and black pepper, to taste

Feta or goat cheese, for garnish

Place a heavy-bottomed saucepan over medium heat and, when it is hot, add the oil. Add the garlic and cook, covered, until golden, about 5 to 7 minutes. Add the spinach and cook until wilted, about 5 to 10 minutes.

Add the stock, raise the heat to high, and bring to a boil. Lower the heat to low, and cook for 10 minutes. Transfer to a container, cover, and refrigerate at least 2 hours and up to 4 hours.

Place the solids in the bowl of a food processor fitted with a steel blade or a blender. Process until smooth, gradually adding the cooking liquid, lemon juice, and yogurt or cream. Add salt and pepper to taste.

Serve immediately, garnished with feta or goat cheese.

YIELD: 6 TO 8 CUPS

Vichyssoise

The classic rich, creamy potato-and-leek soup is served cold, garnished with chopped chives. Created in the United States by a French chef from the Bourbonnais, this beauty really shouldn't be toyed with. I do, however, make one exception: Though the traditional recipe calls for peeled potatoes, I keep the skins on; they add texture and flecks of color.

1 bunch leeks, sliced (3½ to 4 cups)
2 tablespoons unsalted butter
4 medium red bliss potatoes, unpeeled, about 3½ to 4 cups cubed
5 cups chicken stock
¾ cup heavy cream, or ½ cup heavy cream and ¼ cup sour cream
¼ teaspoon ground nutmeg
¼ teaspoon white or black pepper
Kosher salt, to taste
Fresh chives, for garnish

Cut off the root end and 3 inches of green part of leeks, and discard. Quarter leeks lengthwise and slice thinly. Soak them in several changes of water, being careful to get rid of all the sand.

Place a large heavy-bottomed saucepan over medium heat and, when it is hot, add the butter. When the butter has melted, add the leeks and cook until wilted, about 10 to 15 minutes.

Add the potatoes and stock, raise the heat to high, cover, and bring to a boil. Lower the heat to low and cook until the potatoes are tender, about 20 minutes.

Place the solids in a food processor. Process until completely smooth, gradually adding the cooking liquid. Add the cream, nutmeg, and pepper. Add salt to taste. Transfer to a container, cover, and refrigerate at least 4 hours and up to overnight. Garnish with chives.

YIELD: 8 TO 9 CUPS

Cream of Watercress

I can't think of watercress without thinking of elderly ladies eating tea sandwiches made with watercress and cucumber. It seems a very civilized food and this soup is certainly that. The optional ginger adds a kick.

1 tablespoons unsalted butter
1 Spanish onion, chopped
2 teaspoons peeled and finely chopped fresh ginger root (optional)
1 potato, cut in small dice
2½ cups chicken stock
1 cup whole milk
2 bunches watercress, a few branches reserved for garnish
Kosher salt and black pepper
Goat cheese, for garnish (optional)
Lightly toasted walnuts, for garnish (optional)

Place a large pot over medium high heat and, when it is hot, add the butter. Add the onion and ginger, if desired, and cook until tender, about 10 to 15 minutes. Add the potato and stock and bring to a slow boil. Lower the heat and cook until the potato is tender, about 15 minutes. Transfer the solids to a blender and blend until smooth. Add the cooking liquid and milk and blend until smooth. Add the watercress and blend until smooth. Add salt and pepper to taste.

Transfer to a container, cover, and refrigerate at least 2 hours, and up to overnight. Garnish with the reserved watercress branches.

YIELD: 5 TO 6 CUPS

Gazpacho

azpacho is often called "liquid salad" in Spain and, generally, when people speak of *gazpacho* they mean the classic red *gazpacho*: tomatoes, cucumbers, bell peppers, and, traditionally, bread (which I have omitted). In fact, for the first five years that I was in business, the traditional variation was the only *gazpacho* I made. Don't be as hesitant as I was; the other variations are as intriguing as they are refreshing.

Classic Red *Gazpacho*

Although gazpacho *has come to mean almost any cold soup based on tomatoes and cucumbers, the original is from southern Spain and included everything here except for the optional herbs and feta cheese. My version of the classic also substitutes croutons for bread crumbs. The addition of feta cheese makes this a more substantial meal, and its creaminess contrasts nicely with the acidity of the* gazpacho.

1 or 2 English cucumbers, cut into ¼ inch dice

2 large, perfectly ripe, vine-ripened tomatoes, cored and cut into
   ¼ inch dice

1 small red, Vidalia, or Spanish onion, coarsely chopped

2 to 4 garlic cloves, minced

2 red bell peppers, cored, seeded, and cut into ¼ inch dice

2 tablespoons extra-virgin olive oil

3 to 4 tablespoons Sherry or red wine vinegar

3 cups tomato (Welch's) or V8 juice

1 cup ice water

1 to 2 teaspoons cayenne pepper

1 to 2 teaspoons kosher salt

⅓ cup chopped fresh dill, cilantro, or basil leaves, for garnish (optional)

½ cup crumbled feta cheese, for garnish (optional)

2 cups croutons, for garnish (page 177)

Place the cucumbers, tomatoes, onion, garlic, and peppers in a bowl, and toss to combine. Remove half the mixture and place in the bowl of a food processor fitted with a steel blade and pulse 2 to 3 times until chopped and combined. Return to the bowl.

Add the oil, vinegar, tomato juice, water, cayenne, and salt and stir to combine.

Cover and refrigerate at least 2 hours and up to 4 hours.

Garnish with fresh herbs, feta, and croutons.

YIELD: 10 TO 12 CUPS

Avocado and Lime *Gazpacho*

*S*omewhat like Red Gazpacho, *somewhat like guacamole, and somewhat like salsa, this soup will heat you up and cool you down.*

1 English cucumber, chopped or thinly sliced
2 perfectly ripe avocados, pitted, peeled, and chopped
2 large tomatoes, diced
1 green or red bell pepper, cored, seeded, and chopped
2 shallots, finely chopped
2 garlic cloves, pressed or finely chopped
2 to 3 tablespoons chopped fresh cilantro leaves
¼ teaspoon crushed red-pepper flakes
1 tablespoon Sherry or red wine vinegar
Juice of ½ lime
2 cups ice water
Croutons, for garnish (page 177)

Place all the ingredients in a large bowl and stir to combine.

Remove half the solids and place in a food processor. Process briefly. Do not use a blender; this soup should have a chunky texture. Return to the soup.

Transfer to a container, cover, and refrigerate at least 2 hours and up to 4 hours.

Garnish with croutons.

YIELD: 5 TO 5½ CUPS

Grape and Cucumber *Gazpacho*

Slightly sweet and tart, this subtle and atypical gazpacho is very refreshing.

1½ cups small seedless grapes

1 to 1½ English cucumbers, chopped

1½ Granny Smith apples, peeled, cored, and cut in small dice

¼ to ½ red onion, chopped

3 tablespoons chopped fresh dill leaves

2½ to 3 cups buttermilk

1½ cups ice water

1 teaspoon kosher salt

½ teaspoon black pepper

4 radishes, sliced paper thin, for garnish

Place the grapes, cucumbers, apples, and onion in the bowl of a food processor fitted with a steel blade and quickly pulse until well chopped. Transfer to a mixing or serving bowl and add the dill, buttermilk, water, salt, and pepper.

Cover and refrigerate at least 2 hours and up to 4 hours.

Garnish with radishes.

YIELD: ABOUT 8 TO 9 CUPS

Cucumber and Cilantro *Gazpacho*

*D*on't even think of making this without fresh cilantro. And certainly don't think of serving it to anyone who doesn't love cilantro.

1 small red onion, finely chopped
1 green pepper, cored, seeded, and diced
1 English cucumber, diced
2 garlic cloves, pressed or finely chopped
1 orange, peeled, pitted, and finely chopped
¼ cup chopped fresh cilantro leaves
2 cups ice water
1 teaspoon kosher salt, or more, to taste
Croutons, for garnish (page 177)

Place all the ingredients in a large bowl and stir to combine.

Remove half the solids and place in the bowl of a food processor fitted with a steel blade. Do not use a blender. Pulse briefly and return to soup. Transfer to a container, cover, and refrigerate at least 2 hours and up to 4 hours.

Garnish with croutons.

YIELD: 5 TO 5½ CUPS

Orange *Gazpacho*

Similar to the classic recipe, the orange juice and yellow pepper lend this gazpacho a slightly sweeter and mellower flavor.

1 small red onion, finely chopped
1 large, perfectly ripe, vine-ripened tomato, cored and diced
1 yellow bell pepper, cored, seeded, and chopped
1 English cucumber, diced
½ cup tomato juice
½ cup orange juice
Kosher salt
Croutons, for garnish (page 177)

Place all ingredients in a large bowl and stir to combine.

Remove half the solids and place in a food processor. Do not use a blender. Pulse briefly and return to soup. Transfer to a container, cover, and refrigerate at least 2 hours and up to 4 hours.

Garnish with croutons.

YIELD: 4 TO 4½ CUPS

Tropical Fruit *Gazpacho*

Sweet and savory, this rendition is fruitier and tangier than the traditional version.

1 red bell pepper, seeded and diced
1 English cucumber, diced
4 scallions, including greens, trimmed and thinly sliced at an angle
2 ripe tomatoes, diced
1 ripe avocado, diced
1 ripe mango, diced
¾ cup pineapple juice, or more, to taste
2 cups tomato juice, or more, to taste
¼ to ½ cup red wine vinegar
¼ cup chopped fresh basil leaves
Tabasco, to taste
Kosher salt and black pepper, to taste
Croutons, for garnish (page 177)

Place all the ingredients in a large serving bowl and mix to combine. If you want a smoother soup, place half or all of the soup in a blender or a food processor fitted with a steel blade and blend until desired consistency. Cover and refrigerate for at least 2 hours and up to 8 hours.

Garnish with croutons.

YIELD: ABOUT 5 TO 6 CUPS

All-Purpose
Salad Dressings

I am fortunate in having a husband and two children who think that a great dinner consists of soup, salad, and bread. They are not meat-and-potatoes types, and for this I am extremely grateful. I almost never hear complaints and if, for some reason, one of the kids isn't interested in the particular soup I am serving, they are welcome to as much salad and bread as they want and, failing that, a bowl of cereal or yogurt.

Like my children, I am a Caesar devotee and purist, but I can't eat it every single night. What follows is a list of greens that I like to combine and then dress simply. When I don't want just greens, I eat a bit of everything, which is the second list.

GREENS:

Arugula—peppery, very sandy

Belgian endive—bitter and crunchy; great paired with strong, creamy cheeses

Bibb—mild and sweet

Boston—buttery, very soft leaves

Chervil—licorice-y

Chicory (curly endive)—has a nice bite but can be slightly bitter to some

Cress—hot and peppery

Dandelion greens—slightly bitter; good in warm salads

Endive—mild, with a bitter edge; crisp, good paired with watercress or radicchio

Frisee—slightly sweet, slightly bitter; good paired with nuts and cheese

Green oak leaf—slightly grassy

Green chard—spinach-like; good in warm salads

Iceberg—crisp, mild; best eaten on its own with blue-cheese dressing

Mâche (lambs' lettuce)—delicate, slightly nutty flavor, best served alone

Mizuna—mustard-y Japanese green

Mustard greens—crunchy, slightly cabbage-y

Radicchio—slightly peppery, bitter

Red chard—slightly beet-like

Red oak leaf—slightly nutty

Romaine—very crunchy, slightly sweet, nutty

Watercress—peppery, spicy, great with a salad of mixed greens and oranges

OTHER INGREDIENTS TO ADD TO SALADS:

Edible flowers

Fruits—apples, pears, tangerines, peaches, grapefruit

Dried fruits—apricots, raisins, currants, sun-dried cherries

GREEN BEANS AND PEAS

FRESH HERBS—cilantro, basil, parsley, dill

COOKED, COOLED, AND SLICED POTATOES

TOMATOES—cherry, beefsteak, plum, yellow

BELL PEPPERS—green, red, orange, yellow, purple; fresh or
roasted

BERMUDA, WALLA WALLA, OR VIDALIA ONIONS

CHEESES—almost anything, including feta, Parmesan, Cheddar,
blue, and Brie

Balsamic Vinaigrette

An all-purpose vinaigrette that's terrific drizzled on just about all greens, vegetables, and cold tuna or chicken. I also use it for marinating chicken and steak.

2 garlic cloves, chopped (optional)
1 teaspoon Dijon mustard
6 tablespoons balsamic vinegar
⅓ to ¾ cup olive oil, depending on taste
Kosher salt and black pepper, to taste

Place the garlic, mustard, and vinegar in a blender or the bowl of a food processor fitted with a steel blade and process until thoroughly combined. While the machine is running, gradually add the olive oil. Add salt and pepper to taste. Transfer to a container, cover, and refrigerate up to one month.

YIELD: ABOUT 1 TO 1¼ CUPS

Citrus Dressing

An all-purpose salad dressing that adds a clean acidity to just about any salad.

½ cup olive oil
½ cup fresh lemon or lime juice
Kosher salt and black pepper, to taste

Place the oil and juice in a small bottle and shake well. Add salt and pepper to taste. Transfer to a continuer, cover, and refrigerate up to one month.

YIELD: ABOUT ¾ CUP

Sarah Conover's Pesto Dressing

My friend Sarah is one of those natural cooks who can throw ingredients together and turn them into something great. When we were in college, she would whip together pies on the spur of the moment. Whenever I write a cookbook, I ask her for recipes and, inevitably, she comes up with something that sounds strange but is amazing.

1 garlic clove
1 tablespoon pine nuts
1 tablespoon grated Parmesan cheese
3 tablespoons chopped fresh basil leaves
¼ cup mayonnaise
¼ cup white wine vinegar
2 tablespoons olive oil
Kosher salt and black pepper, to taste

Place the garlic, pine nuts, Parmesan cheese, and basil in a blender or the bowl of a food processor fitted with a steel blade and process until thoroughly combined. While the machine is running, gradually add the mayonnaise, vinegar, and olive oil. Add salt and pepper to taste. Transfer to a container, cover, and refrigerate up to one month.

YIELD: ¾ CUP

Orange Vinaigrette

This light vinaigrette is wonderful on romaine salad with endive, yellow peppers, tomatoes, cucumbers, peaches, and goat cheese or on arugula with thinly sliced red onions.

---

3 tablespoons Sherry vinegar or 2 tablespoons red wine vinegar
and 1 tablespoon Sherry
2 tablespoons fresh orange juice
Grated zest of 1 orange (about ¾ to 1 teaspoon)
4 to 5 tablespoons olive oil
Kosher salt and black pepper, to taste

Place the vinegar, orange juice, and zest in a blender or the bowl of a food processor fitted with a steel blade, and process until thoroughly combined. While the machine is running, gradually add the olive oil. Add salt and pepper to taste. Transfer to a continuer, cover, and refrigerate up to one month.

YIELD: ABOUT ¾ CUP

Creamy Blue Cheese

I grew up eating salads with the kind of chunky blue cheese dressing served at steak houses and, although I really love thick, rich, creamy blue cheese dressing, it's always seemed like too much of a splurge to eat at home. However, since soup is mostly broth and therefore low in calories, eating a pile of lettuce with creamy blue cheese dressing only evens things out!

Best to eat on romaine or iceberg lettuce, or with cut-up vegetables.

½ cup crumbled blue cheese
¼ cup buttermilk
¼ cup whole milk yogurt, taken from the creamy top, if possible
2 teaspoons fresh lemon juice
Pinch sugar
Kosher salt and black pepper, to taste

Place the blue cheese in a bowl and mash with a fork until it is crumbly but not creamy. Add the buttermilk and yogurt and continue mashing. Add the lemon juice and sugar, mix to combine. Add salt and pepper to taste. Transfer to a container, cover, and refrigerate at least 1 hour, and up to one week.

YIELD: ABOUT 1¼ CUPS

Stan Frankenthaler's
Green Goddess Dressing

This classic dressing, from Boston chef Stan Frankenthaler, is great on soft lettuces like Bibb or red leaf.

1 garlic clove
2 to 3 anchovy fillets
1 tablespoon capers
½ cup flat-leaf spinach leaves
2 scallions, chopped
¼ cup Italian flat-leaf parsley leaves
2 tablespoons chopped fresh tarragon leaves
¼ cup sour cream
½ cup mayonnaise
1 teaspoon aged white vinegar
½ teaspoon kosher salt
¼ teaspoon black pepper

Place the garlic, anchovy fillets, capers, spinach, scallions, parsley, and tarragon in a blender or food processor fitted with a steel blade and process until smooth. Add the sour cream and blend until smooth. Stir in the mayonnaise, vinegar, salt, and pepper. Transfer to a container, cover, and refrigerate up to one week.

YIELD: ¾ TO 1 CUP

Caesar Dressing

Although Caesar salad is traditionally made at the table or in the kitchen just prior to serving, my family eats so much of it that I like to have the dressing on hand. The truth is that Lauren and Ben ask for it nightly and, like the countless children I have fed it to, they inevitably wolf it down. It has just the sweet, salty, crunchy combination children love so much.

4 garlic cloves
2 to 3 anchovy fillets
½ teaspoon Dijon mustard
½ cup fresh lemon juice (about 2 lemons)
¼ to ½ cup grated or shaved Parmesan cheese
½ cup olive oil
Kosher salt and black pepper, to taste

Place everything except for the olive oil and Parmesan in a blender or a food processor fitted with a steel blade, and process until thoroughly combined. While the machine is running, gradually add the olive oil. Add salt and pepper, to taste.

Either add the Parmesan to the salad after it is dressed or add it after the olive oil. Transfer to a container, cover, and refrigerate up to one month.

YIELD: ABOUT 1 CUP

Breads to Make It a Meal

GREAT SANDWICHES TO EAT WITH SOUP:

Turkey, avocado, and bacon
Turkey, stuffing, and cranberry sauce or chutney
Turkey, Brie cheese, and curried mayonnaise
Fresh tomatoes, mozzarella, and fresh basil leaves
Avocado, tomato, and cheddar cheese
Roasted vegetables with or without goat cheese,
mozzarella, or Brie cheese
Roasted vegetables with pesto
Assorted cheeses and pesto, with or without tomatoes
Caramelized onions and cream cheese
Roasted peppers and mozzarella, with or without pesto
Goat cheese and pears or apples
Pesto, mozzarella, and tomatoes
Tomatoes and mayonnaise
Guacamole and cheddar cheese

ADD-ONS TO ANY SANDWICH:

Carrots (sliced with a vegetable peeler)
Cucumbers, thinly sliced
Radishes, thinly sliced
Apples, peaches, or pears, thinly sliced
Fresh basil leaves
Greens

Croutons

Whenever I have bread ends I dice them, and throw them in a plastic zipper bag in the freezer. When they accumulate, I make croutons, which I add to salads and soups for an ineffable crunch.

4 to 5 cups ½-inch bread cubes

2 tablespoons olive oil

2 garlic cloves, minced

1 teaspoon kosher salt

1 tablespoon finely grated Parmesan or Asiago cheese

Preheat the oven to 350 degrees.

Place the bread, oil, garlic, salt, and cheese in a bowl, and toss to combine. Transfer to a baking sheet and bake until just golden, about 15 to 20 minutes. Set aside to cool. Use immediately or transfer to a plastic zipper bag and freeze up to two months.

YIELD: 4 TO 5 CUPS

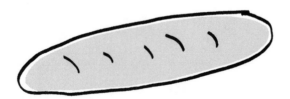

Cornbread

I am on a constant quest for perfect cornbread, wanting one that's moist and not too sweet. This Northern–Southern combo is as close as I have ever come. It's great slathered with unsalted butter and honey.

1¼ cups yellow stone-ground cornmeal
1¼ cups all-purpose flour
2 teaspoons baking powder
1 teaspoon kosher salt
2 tablespoons sugar or honey
2 large eggs, lightly beaten
1½ cups buttermilk, yogurt, or sour cream
4 tablespoons unsalted butter, melted

Preheat the oven to 350 degrees. Lightly grease an 8-inch square baking pan or a 8-inch cast-iron skillet.

Place the cornmeal, flour, baking powder, salt, and sugar in a large mixing bowl. Make a well in the center and add the eggs, yogurt, and butter. Mix the wet ingredients together. Mix in the dry ingredients until just blended.

Spoon the batter into the prepared pan and bake until it just begins to color, about 30 to 35 minutes. Do not let it brown. Serve hot or at room temperature.

YIELD: 9 GENEROUS PIECES

VARIATIONS:

Cheddar Cornbread: **Add ½ to ⅔ cup shredded Cheddar cheese with the wet ingredients.**

Chipotle Cornbread: **Add 1 or 2 chopped chipotle chilies packed in adobo, rinsed, with the wet ingredients.**

Irish Soda Bread

An old standby from college, there isn't a soup this bread doesn't pair well with. I have altered the dry ingredients almost yearly. You can certainly substitute almost any flour, as well as ingredients like soy powder, to suit your tastes. This is my latest favorite. It is very crumbly and not partial to keeping.

1 cup all-purpose flour
½ cup rolled oats
¼ cup stone-ground cornmeal
¼ cup wheat germ
1½ teaspoons baking powder
1 teaspoon kosher salt
1 teaspoon sugar
½ teaspoon baking soda
4 tablespoons unsalted butter, chilled or frozen, in thin slices
1 tablespoon caraway seeds (optional)
½ cup currants (optional)
1 large egg
¾ cup buttermilk
1 large egg yolk, beaten

Preheat the oven to 375 degrees. Line a baking sheet with parchment paper.

Place the flour, oats, cornmeal, wheat germ, baking powder, salt, sugar, and baking soda in the bowl of a food processor fitted with a steel blade and pulse to combine. While the processor is running, add the butter, a few slices at a time, and process until the mixture resembles cornmeal. Add the caraway seeds and/or currants, if desired.

Place the egg and buttermilk in a large mixing bowl and mix to combine. Add the flour mixture and mix, *by hand*, until combined. Form into a ball, place on the prepared sheet, and flatten down a bit. Using the tip of a sharp knife, make an x in the top, then brush with egg yolk. Transfer to

continued on next page

Irish Soda Bread (*cont.*)

the oven and bake until the bottom sounds hollow when tapped and the top is golden brown, about 30 minutes. Serve immediately.

YIELD: 1 LOAF

Biscuits

Light, airy, buttery, and crispy on the outside. The first time that I made these perfect biscuits, both Lauren and I ate four. I thought they were so good hot, they wouldn't be good when they had cooled. Boy, was I wrong!

---

3 cups all-purpose flour
1 tablespoon sugar
1 tablespoon baking powder
1 teaspoon kosher salt
1 teaspoon baking soda
12 tablespoons unsalted butter, chilled or frozen, in thin slices
1 cup buttermilk

Preheat the oven to 425 degrees. Line a baking sheet with parchment paper.

Place the flour, sugar, baking powder, salt, and baking soda in the bowl of a food processor fitted with a steel blade and pulse to combine. While the processor is running, add the butter, a few slices at a time, and process until the mixture resembles cornmeal. Transfer the mixture to a large mixing bowl, add the buttermilk and mix, *by hand*, until combined. Divide the mixture into 12 pieces and place on the prepared baking sheet. Transfer to the oven and bake until golden brown, about 12 to 15 minutes. Serve immediately.

YIELD: 12 BISCUITS

Garlic Bread

This mixture can also be dolloped on soups or grilled clams, or mixed into noodles.

¼ cup olive oil
8 to 10 garlic cloves, minced or chopped
½ cup unsalted butter, at room temperature
½ teaspoon dried Greek oregano
1 teaspoon kosher salt
1 tablespoon chopped fresh basil leaves (optional)
1 tablespoon chopped fresh cilantro leaves (optional)
1 French or Italian baguette, sliced and lightly toasted
Grated Parmesan cheese (optional)

Place a large skillet over very low heat and add the olive oil. Add the garlic and cook until tender and lightly colored, about 10 minutes. Do not let it brown. Set aside to cool for 10 minutes. Off heat, add the butter, and combine well. Add the oregano and salt. Add the basil and cilantro, if desired. Transfer to a small serving bowl and, if not using immediately, cover and refrigerate.

Place the toast in a basket and serve immediately. Spread the butter on the toast and sprinkle with Parmesan cheese, if desired.

YIELD: ABOUT ⅔ CUP

Seven Perfect Sweets

My idea of a great dessert—both to make and to eat—is a very simple one. Any of these will finish a soup meal perfectly.

Cocoa Cookies

Almost black, really rich, slightly crunchy, these are among my absolute favorite cookies. Make a big batch and store the dough, or the cookies themselves, in the freezer. They taste great frozen too.

Feel free to add chocolate chips, broken-up peppermint sticks, or to substitute pecans, almonds, or peanuts for the walnuts.

½ pound (2 sticks) unsalted butter, at room temperature

2 cups sugar

2 large eggs, at room temperature

1 tablespoon vanilla extract

2 cups all-purpose flour

1 cup unsweetened cocoa powder

1 teaspoon baking soda

½ teaspoon baking powder

½ teaspoon kosher salt

1½ cups toasted walnuts

Preheat the oven to 350 degrees. Lightly grease a cookie sheet and line it with parchment paper.

Place the butter and sugar in the bowl of a mixer fitted with a paddle, and mix until smooth. Scrape down the sides of the bowl, add the eggs and vanilla, and mix until just combined, being careful not to overbeat. Scrape down the sides of the bowl, add the flour, cocoa powder, baking soda, baking powder, salt, and, if desired, walnuts, and mix until well blended.

Place teaspoonsful on the prepared cookie sheet and transfer to the oven. Bake until the edges begin to firm up, about 12 to 14 minutes. Do not overbake. For crispy cookies, let cool on the sheet. Cool the cookie sheet between batches.

YIELD: ABOUT 5 DOZEN

Toasted Hazelnut Shortbread Cookies

Buttery, crumbly, and nutty, these cookies are perfect with tea. (When eaten after soup, that is.)

½ pound (2 sticks) unsalted butter, at room temperature
⅓ cup white sugar
¼ cup brown sugar
1 teaspoon vanilla extract
1 cup lightly toasted hazelnuts, about ¾ cup, finely ground
2 cups all-purpose flour
1 teaspoon kosher salt
¼ cup confectioners' sugar, for sprinkling

Place the butter and sugars in the bowl of a mixer fitted with a paddle and mix until smooth. Scrape down the sides of the bowl, add the vanilla and hazelnuts, and mix until light and fluffy. Scrape down the sides of the bowl, add the flour and salt, and mix until well blended. The batter will seem excessively dry, but that's the way it's supposed to be.

Form the dough into a ball, cover with plastic wrap, and refrigerate for at least ½ hour and up to two days.

Preheat the oven to 350 degrees.

To form the cookies, break off into small pieces and roll into balls. Place on an ungreased cookie sheet and transfer to the oven. Bake until the edges just begin to brown, about 12 to 14 minutes. Cool for 2 minutes, remove to a wire rack, and sprinkle with confectioners' sugar. Cool the baking sheet between batches.

YIELD: ABOUT 3 TO 4 DOZEN COOKIES

Brownies

Although most people will find this hard to do, these brownies are truly best after they have been refrigerated for at least a few hours and ideally, overnight. If you must, cut off one small piece, then refrigerate the remainder—but remember, I warned you.

Scharffen Berger Chocolate, available at specialty shops or on the internet (www.scharffenberger.com) is definitely my chocolate of choice for this recipe.

To hasten the cooling of the chocolate, place the saucepan in a larger pan or bowl of cold water. Stir occasionally.

---

12 tablespoons unsalted butter

6 ounces semisweet or bittersweet chocolate

3 ounces unsweetened chocolate

3 large eggs, at room temperature

1 tablespoon vanilla extract

1 cup plus 2 tablespoons sugar

½ teaspoon kosher salt

1 cup all-purpose flour

1 to 1½ cups coarsely chopped walnuts or pecans (optional)

Preheat the oven to 350 degrees. Butter and flour a 9 x 13 inch baking pan.

Place the butter and chocolates in a saucepan and cook, stirring constantly, over the lowest possible heat until both are melted, about 3 to 5 minutes. Set aside to cool.

Place the eggs, vanilla, and sugar in a large mixing bowl, and stir until just combined. Add the chocolate mixture, and stir until just combined. Add the salt and flour and stir until well combined. Pour into the prepared pan and sprinkle with the nuts, if desired. Transfer to the oven and cook until your kitchen smells like chocolate and a toothpick inserted in the pan comes out clean, about 25 to 30 minutes. Set aside to cool, then refrigerate at least 4 hours, and up to overnight.

YIELD: ABOUT 24 BROWNIES

Oatmeal Lace Cookies

More delicate and light than the typical oatmeal cookie.

½ cup unsalted butter, at room temperature
1 cup sugar
1 tablespoon vanilla extract
¼ cup all-purpose flour
1½ cups rolled oats
¼ teaspoon kosher salt

Preheat the oven to 350 degrees. Line a baking sheet with parchment paper.

Place the butter and sugar in the bowl of a mixer fitted with a paddle, or the bowl of a food processor fitted with a mixing blade, and mix until creamy. Scrape down the sides of the bowl, add the remaining ingredients, and scrape again.

Place teaspoonsful 2 inches apart on the prepared sheet, and bake until golden brown, about 10 to 12 minutes. Allow the cookies to set on the sheet for no more than 2 minutes, then transfer to a rack.

YIELD: ABOUT 36 COOKIES

Milly Romanzi's Fruit Tart

One night Mark and I were at our friends Ken and Milly Romanzi's home, when Milly decided to whip up dessert. Ken is really the cook in their household, so I was amazed to watch Milly effortlessly offer up this absolutely wonderful and easy masterpiece. I wish she'd made two. You can use any fruit that is in season.

For the dough:

> 1 cup all-purpose flour
> ¼ teaspoon kosher salt
> ¼ teaspoon sugar
> 6 tablespoons unsalted butter, chilled or frozen, cut into 12 pieces
> Ice water, up to ¼ cup

For the filling:

> 2¼ tablespoons all-purpose flour
> 3 plus 6 plus 4 tablespoons sugar
> 6 to 8 plums, pears, peaches or apricots, very thinly sliced

Preheat the oven to 400 degrees.

To make the dough: Place the flour, salt, sugar, and butter in a bowl, and knead by hand until the dough looks like little pills. Add the water, one tablespoon at a time, and form into a ball. Flatten into a large disc, cover with plastic wrap, and refrigerate for one hour.

To assemble the tart: Using a rolling pin, roll the dough into a 15-inch circle on a big piece of aluminum foil. Sprinkle the flour and 3 tablespoons sugar in the center, leaving a 2-inch border all around. Overlap the fruit slices so that, in the end, the thickness is about 2 to 3 slices throughout. Sprinkle the top with 6 tablespoons sugar. Fold up the border to partially cover the fruit, and pinch and seal the corners where possible. Brush the top with water and sprinkle the remaining 4 tablespoons sugar on the top. Transfer to the oven and bake until the top is lightly browned and the fruit is bubbling, at least 35, and up to 50, minutes. Serve immediately.

YIELD: 4 SERVINGS

James Mauch's Fruit Crisp

I call this James Mauch's Fruit Crisp not because he gave me the recipe but because, when I gave it to him, he became obsessed. When I went to visit James and his wife, Sharon, he insisted that I teach him to make this. Actually, what I did was simply order him around his own kitchen. (What fun!) Now he is an aficionado and I can't make a crisp without thinking of James. His virgin run was with strawberries and rhubarb (my favorite); Sharon's daughter Hilary ate three portions and daughter Alexandra ate it for breakfast. We just didn't tell them about the rhubarb.

I always seem to include a recipe for fruit crisp in my cookbooks and, with each new recipe, I like to think I've improved upon the last. This, the latest incarnation, is probably the last one, because it is perfectly balanced in flavor and texture.

> ✳ MEANING "ROOT OF THE BARBARIANS," **RHUBARB** IS TECHNICALLY A VEGETABLE, BUT IS USED AS, AND CONSIDERED, A FRUIT. ORIGINALLY USED AS A DECORATIVE AND MEDICINAL PLANT, RHUBARB WAS DISCOVERED AS A FOOD BY EUROPEANS IN THE EIGHTEENTH CENTURY. THE LEAVES, ALTHOUGH BEAUTIFUL, ARE TOXIC AND SHOULD NEVER BE EATEN; THE STALKS ARE VERY ACIDIC, WHICH MAKES THEM PERFECT FOR PAIRING WITH FRUIT AND SUGAR.

1 cup plus 2 tablespoons all-purpose flour
1 cup plus 2 tablespoons rolled oats
1 cup pecans or walnuts (optional)
¼ cup white sugar
⅓ cup brown sugar
½ teaspoon kosher salt
½ cup unsalted butter, melted

Place the flour, oats, nuts, if desired, sugars, and salt in a large mixing bowl and toss together. Add the butter and toss again.

continued on next page

James Mauch's Fruit Cup (*cont.*)

Fill an 8 x 8 inch pan with fruit, and then top with the crisp ingredients.

OPTIONS FOR THE FRUIT:

1 tablespoon all-purpose flour and 1 to 2 tablespoons sugar plus 4 to 6 cups of any of the following:

   Apples
   Pears
   Strawberry and Rhubarb
   Peaches
   Peaches and Blueberries
   Berries

Bread Pudding with Whisky and White Chocolate

Instead of eating bread with your soup, save it for dessert. Bread pudding tends to be either mostly custard or mostly bread, which is the way I like it: this one has a crispy crust, dense interior, isn't too eggy, and is just sweet but not too sweet. It is definitely rich—a little like French toast grown up.

½ cup plus ¼ cup sugar
4 large eggs
2 large egg yolks
2 cups heavy cream
1 cup milk
2 teaspoons vanilla extract
¼ cup whisky
4 ounces white chocolate, finely grated
½ loaf day-old challah (about 5 to 6 cups cubed)

Preheat the oven to 350 degrees. Butter a 9-inch loaf pan or an 8 x 8 inch pan. Fill a 10 x 13 inch pan with one inch of water.

Place ½ cup sugar, eggs, egg yolks, cream, milk, vanilla, whisky, and white chocolate in a large mixing bowl and mix well. Add the bread cubes and submerge them in the mixture. Let sit for 10 minutes. Transfer to the prepared pan and sprinkle the remaining ¼ cup sugar over the top. Place the pan into the larger pan filled with water. Transfer to the oven, and bake until the pudding is set and golden brown, about 45 minutes to 1 hour. Set aside to cool for 15 minutes. Serve warm or at room temperature.

Index

Geller, Helen, 102
ginger:
    Butternut Squash with Lime, Garlic and, 24
    Carrot with Cream, 37
    Chicken with Dill and, Carol Lessor's, 96
    Cilantro with Cream, 35
    Melon, 145
    Vietnamese Chicken with Lots of Accompaniments, 109
goat cheese:
    Broccoli with, 12
    Tomato with, 63
Gordon Hamersley's Lentil, 89
Gordon Hamersley's Roasted Vegetable Stew with Garlic Crumble Crust, 134–35
Grape and Cucumber *Gazpacho,* 162
Greek flavors, in *Avgolemono,* 95
Green Goddess Dressing, Stan Frankenthaler's, 174
greens:
    Beet, Beets, and Lentils, 42
    Collard, Black-Eyed Pea with, 74–75
    for salads, 167
    see also romaine; spinach
Grilled Asparagus with White Beans and Prosciutto, David Filippetti's, 93

H

ham:
    Black Bean with Vegetables and, 87–88
    Prosciutto, Grilled Asparagus with White Beans and, David Filippetti's, 93
    Vegetable with Romaine, Parmesan and, Pattie Sampson's, 108
Hamersley, Gordon, 89, 134
Harpoon Chili, 124–25
Harvest Restaurant (Cambridge, Mass.), 87
hazelnut:
    Frangelico, Mushroom with, 54
    Toasted, Shortbread Cookies, 185
Helen Geller's Matzoh Ball, 102–3
herbes de Provence, 89
    Lentil, Gordon Hamersley's, 89
herbs:
    dried, xviii–xix
    fresh, xix
    Fresh, Asparagus with, 6–7
    Vegetable Stew with Raisins, Rice and, Moroccan, 130–31
    see also specific herbs
honeydew, in Ginger Melon, 145
Hunter's Soup, 52–53

I

iceberg lettuce, 167
Indian flavors:
    Mulligatawny, 105–6
    Spicy Cauliflower, 26
    see also curry(ied)
ingredients, xvii–xix
    dried herbs and spices, xviii–xix
    general equivalents for, xv–xvi
    pantry, essential, xvii–xviii
Irish Soda Bread, 179–80
Italian flavors:
    Fennel *Minestrone,* 68
    Noah Levin's *Minestrone,* 71
    Pappa al Pomodoro, 60
    Pasta e Fagioli, 81–82
    Ribollita (Tuscan *Minestrone*), 69–70
    Summer *Minestrone,* 152–53

J

James Mauch's Fruit Crisp, 189–90
Jewish classics:
    Chicken with Ginger and Dill, Carol Lessor's, 96
    Matzoh Ball, Helen Geller's, 102–3

K

kale, xvi, 76
    Cape Cod, 84–85
    and *Chorizo,* Portuguese *(Caldo Verde),* 65
    Lentil and, 76–77
    Ribollita (Tuscan *Minestrone*), 69–70
    White Bean and, 75
kidney beans:
    Beef Chili with Beer, 119–20
    Chili with Eggplant and Beef, 122–23
    Harpoon Chili, 124–25
    Minestrone, Noah Levin's, 71
    Pasta e Fagioli, 81–82
    Three Bean, 91

L

Lace Cookies, Oatmeal, 187
lambs' lettuce (mâche), 167
leek(s), xvi
    Mushroom, Barley and, 45
    Vichyssoise, 157
lemon:
    Artichoke, 16–17
    Avgolemono, 95
    Spinach with Garlic, Yogurt and, 156
    Split Pea with, 86
    Zest, Chicken with Thyme, Potatoes and, 101